Islamic manners

Abd al-Fattah
Abu Ghuddah

Islamic manners

Abd al-Fattah
Abu Ghuddah

TRANSLATED BY

MUHAMMAD ZAHID ABU GHUDDAH

CLARITAS
BOOKS

1 2 3 4 5 6 7 8 9 10

Claritas Books

Bernard Street, Swansea, United Kingdom
Milpitas, California, United States

CLARITAS
BOOKS

First edition: May 2001 / Rabīᶜ al-Awwal 1422
Second edition: June 2003 / Rabīᶜ al-Awwal 1424
Third edition: July 2007 / Rajab 1428

Typeset in Bembo 11/14

Islamic Manners
by Abd al-Fattah Abu Ghuddah
Translated by Muhammad Zahid Abu Ghuddah
Editied by Sharif H Banna

A CIP catalogue record for this book is available from the British Library

ISBN: 9780953758272

Special thanks to
Wassim, Ayman, Hiba, Attia, Abdul Basit, Alia,
Muazzem, Nadim, and Jilani

بسم الله الرحمن الرحيم

SHAYKH ʿABD AL-FATTĀḤ ABŪ GHUDDAH was born in Syria in 1917. One of the outstanding Muslim scholars of the 20th century, Shaykh Abū Ghuddah was a leading scholar in the field of hadith and Ḥanafī school of Fiqh. He studied in Syria and Egypt specialising in Arabic language, hadith, sharīʿah and psychology. He had many prominent teachers, among them Shaykh Rāghib al-Tabbākh, Shaykh Aḥmad ibn Muḥammad al-Zarqa, Shaykh ʿĪsā al-Bayanūnī, Shaykh Aḥmad al-Kurdī, and the renowned Ottoman Scholar Imām al-Kawtharī. He taught Uṣūl al-Fiqh, Ḥanafī Fiqh and Comparitive Fiqh at the University of Damascus. He also taught at the King Saud University and Imām Muhammad ibn Saud Islamic University. He was buried in al-Baki' cemetery in Madinah 1997.

CONTENTS

FOREWORD

All praises are for Allah, Lord and Sustainer of the universe. May the peace and blessings of Allah be upon our beloved Messenger Muḥammad, his family and his righteous Companions.

Ibn al-Mubārak said, "Mukhlid Ibn al-Ḥusayn once said to me, 'We are more in need of acquiring *adab* than learning hadith.'" If this statement was true several centuries ago, then it is more true now. The mere acquisition of knowledge alone is insufficient to build a sound and balanced Islamic personality. Imām Zakariyya al-Anṣārī once said, "Knowledge without *adab* is like fire without wood and *adab* without knowledge is like a spirit without a body."

Imām Ibn al-Qayyim quoted the early sufis as saying, "*Taṣawwuf* is good manners, and anyone who surpasses you in manners is better than you in *taṣawwuf*." Ibn al-Qayyim comments on this by saying, "Indeed, the *dīn* [of Islam] itself is manners; anyone surpassing you in manners is better than you in the *dīn*." This is true, for we need only to quote the hadith as related in Bukhārī wherein the Prophet ﷺ says, "I have not been sent [as a Messenger] except to perfect morals."

Adab or manners is an integral part of the development of a sound Islamic personality. It is something that one is brought up with, sees around him and thus acquires it. The beauty of a civilisation is manifested in the values and manners embodied in the interaction of its members. The more dignified the manners, the more stable and vibrant the social fabric of a society. But sadly, we live in times where *adab* is lacking at all levels of society. We live in a "*adab*-less" society where parents are disrespected, teachers are not treated with due honour, elders are not given their due rights and the basic manners of eating, visiting, appearance and conversation are not observed. So sad is the predicament that books have to be written and lectures have to be delivered in order to teach *adab*. Traditionally, *adab* was not something that was formally "taught." Rather, it was something "acquired" and embodied in the very interaction between people.

Such is the importance of manners, trivial though they may seem, that the actions of a believer will be rendered null void if manners are lacking. In the Quran, Allah the Exalted, addressing the Companions of the Prophet ﷺ and says, *O you who believe, raise not your voices above the voice of the Prophet, nor speak aloud to him in talk as you speak to one another, lest your deeds may be rendered fruitless while you perceive not* (Quran, 49:2).

Imām Bukhārī reported that ʿAbdullāh ibn al Zubayr said that after the revelation of this verse, whenever ʿUmar ibn al-Khaṭṭāb wanted to speak to the Prophet ﷺ, he would talk almost in whispers to the point that the Prophet ﷺ could hardly hear him and would ask him to repeat what he said. Such was his eagerness in abiding by the *adab* of conversation lest his righteous actions become unaccepted by Allah.

Many of the Muslims, especially the youth of today, are not ill-mannered because of intentionally failing to abide by basic manners, but because they are truly ignorant of what manners are. We live in societies that emphasize material progress and fail to even consider the role of ethics, values, spirituality, character-building and manners. Hence, we are in need of reminding ourselves of the *adab* that should be embodied in our personalities.

However, *adab* should also not be viewed as a separate entity detached from other aspects of life. It should be seen as the *essence* of all work, especially the work of *daʿwa* and striving to change society. To go to an extreme by claiming that *adab* is all that is required is also a gross injustice.

Once, whilst visiting a Muslim country, I attended a lecture of a prominent Islamic figure who was discussing in great detail the *adab* of standing and sitting. Upon enquiry, I learned that the topic of *adab* was the subject matter of nearly every lecture delivered by many of the prominent Islamic figures of that country. The day-to-day problems of society were being neglected. Few spoke against the rule of tyranny, oppression and injustice. Social, economic and political problems were not being addressed or even highlighted. *Adab* is certainly important, but neglecting other vital aspects of life is surely not part of the comprehensive methodology of Islam. Prof. Khuram Murad (1932-1996), a leader and thinker of the Islamic Movement once said:

> Life has many dimensions, many layers, many phases: all of them should be viewed together, in continuing dynamic interaction with each other. For life is an integrated whole. It would be folly to atomise and analyse life as to end up looking at it through a microscope, seeing only one dimension at a time, magnified disproportionately; or with a telescope, resulting in simplistic reductionism. To employ tunnel vision is to live with an unbalanced concern for one aspect and a disregard for others. In all ages men have committed this folly, but perhaps never on the same scale as today. The consequences of this disproportion and imbalance are disastrous: disintegration of person and society, as one lives in one dimension alone or in disregard of the wholeness of life.

This book was written by Shaykh Abū Ghuddah and translated by his son Prof. Muhammad Zahid Abū Ghuddah. The likes of Shaykh Abū Ghuddah are rare to come by. He was one of the most prominent scholars of hadith in the 20th Century and a leader of the Islamic Movement in Syria, thus striving not only in narrating Prophetic traditions but also making them a living reality. He was put into prison in 1966 because of his struggle to establish Islam in all spheres of society. He would often say, "I do not care when I am killed as a Muslim, whichever side takes a wound for Allah."

Shaykh Abū Ghuddah chose to write on this topic because he observed many people disregarding these essential *adab* or misinterpreting them. It is thus indeed an honour for Awakening Publications to publish such a book, on such a topic and written by such a person.

S. M. Ḥasan Al-Banna
May 2001, London

TRANSLATOR'S INTRODUCTION

The best of praise is for Allah and the complete prayers for His Messenger Muḥammad ﷺ, the merciful gift of Allah to humanity.

This book exemplifies the character of the author, my respected father. In his manners and style, he was as perfect as humans could be in following the example of the Prophet ﷺ whom Allah portrayed in the Quran, *Truly, you have the best of manners* (Quran, 68:4).

My father was a very discerning observer noticing the slightest *faux pas* in manners and style, and he enjoyed a fine aesthetic sense of putting every item, whether a sofa or a pair of shoes in its right place. May Allah bless him. He was very keen to instil these graceful manners in those around him: his children, his grandchildren and his students. Appearance was not less important for him despite his extreme humbleness. You could not find a fault with his trimmed and combed beard and moustache, clipped nails, crisp clean clothes and spotless shining shoes. When you approach him, you enjoy the fragrance of his favourite scent, specially formulated for him by a faithful perfumer in Aleppo, the city that loved him beyond imagination.

This book was dear to his heart because he felt that Muslims possess a great wealth in manners and styles manifest in the life of our Prophet ﷺ and the lives of his Companions, as well as the lives of the great Muslim scholars with whose biographies he lived most of his life. This book will enable you to gain insightful glimpses to his personality and manners and his dedication to share it with his Muslim brothers and sisters and see them applying it to all aspects of their lives.

Although this is the first translation of this book, there were writers who wrote on this subject using the Arabic edition extensively with total disregard to intellectual rights. This translation is an extended version of the first Arabic edition; about one third of it is new material from my father's notes and additions. The *aḥadīth* cited are annotated, and the Arabic names were written based, with some modifications based on the Chicago Manual of Style.

I would like to thank those who reviewed the translation and shared their valuable comments, notably sister Heba Attia and brother Abdul Basit Khan. May Allah reward them. I would appreciate hearing from the readers their comments and suggestions. I also call upon the friends of my father, may Allah bless his soul, to share with us stories, anecdotes, photos, tapes and videotapes so that it may be included in a forthcoming book fully dedicated to his great life.

I pray to Allah for the best of rewards for our Prophet ﷺ, his heirs—the scholars of Islam—and those who follow their path to happiness and salvation in this life and in the Hereafter. Ameen.

Muhammad Zahid Abū Ghuddah
December 2000, Toronto, Canada

PREFACE

The best of praise and glory is to Allah, the Lord of the universe. May the best of prayers and peace be on Allah's Messenger Muḥammad, his family, his Companions and his pious followers who follow his guidance and etiquette. O Allah! Guide us to follow them in what we say and what we do until we leave this life.

This is a small book on the manners of Islam in which I have collected selected texts on this important subject. The hadiths cited in this book are either *ṣaḥīḥ* [authentic] or *ḥasan* [good].

I wrote this book because I have seen many of my beloved brothers and sisters disregard these manners and misinterpret them. In compiling it, I hope to remind them of these manners. I do not claim to be better or less in need of practicing these manners; but it is the duty of enjoining good and forbidding evil and observing the commands of Allah: *And remind [them], for a reminder benefits the believers* (Quran, 51:55).

May Allah enable all of us to benefit from good reminders and make this of benefit to my readers and myself. May Allah protect us and be our guide in this life and in the Hereafter.

Shaykh ʿAbd al-Fattaḥ Abū Ghuddah
1 Muharram 1412, Riyadh, Saudi Arabia

Chapter One

THE SCOPE OF ISLAMIC MANNERS

The religion of Islam has rules of etiquette and manners covering every aspect of life. These are applicable for the whole society: the old and the young, men and women. We must not forget that the Prophet ﷺ said, "Women are the counterparts of men."[1] Hence, what is required of men, in adhering to Islamic manners, is likewise required of women; for together they form the Muslim society and through them Islam is introduced and identified.

These manners cover even minor acts, such as entering or exiting a bathroom, posture while sitting and cleaning oneself. At the time of the Prophet ﷺ, one of the polytheists mockingly said to Salmān al-Fārisī, "Your prophet has taught you everything, even the manners of going to the toilet." Salmān answered, "Yes, the Prophet ﷺ forbade us from facing the *qibla* (direction of Kaʿba) when urinating or relieving ourselves." Salmān continued, "The Prophet ﷺ asked us not to use the right hand when cleaning ourselves and to use at least three stones for cleaning."[2]

Islam advocates these etiquette and stresses it so as to perfect the Islamic personality and to bring about harmony among people. There is no doubt that embodying such manners and virtues enhances personal style and qualities, refines the character and brings us closer to the hearts and minds of others. Also, it makes life easier as we know what to do and what to expect from others.

The following manners and etiquette are central to Islam, its purposes and its aims. Calling it "etiquette" by no means implies that it is marginal to life and social behaviour. It does not mean Muslims have the option of ignoring their code of behaviour or that it is merely preferable to adhere to it.

In pointing out that manners rank higher than deeds, Imām al-Qarāfī in his book *al-Furūq* said, "You should know that a little of good manners is better than a lot of good actions."[3] Ruwaym, the righteous scholar, told his son, "Oh my son, make your deeds salt and your manners flour." Many good manners with few good deeds are better than many good deeds with few good manners.

Even if some of these rules appear to be simple common courtesy, it is important to highlight their significance in social behaviour. They provide socially accepted norms for dealing with various activities and functions. By following them, we attain consistency confidence and avoid confusion.

Chapter Two

THE IMPORTANCE OF APPEARANCE

2.1 The Distinct Muslim Personality

The Muslim personality is a distinct one due to its unique code of behaviour and manners. Your appearance, taste, manners, and character reflect your personality. Our master,[4] the Messenger of Allah ﷺ, directed the blessed Companions by saying, "You are on your way to meet your brothers, put on nice dress and fix your saddles[5] so you appear distinct among people as a beauty mark[6] [on a beautiful face]. Allah likes neither roughness nor rough manners."[7]

When the Prophet ﷺ said, "He will not enter Paradise who has a grain of arrogance in his heart," a man asked, "A man may like his dress to be nice and his shoes to be nice." The Prophet ﷺ answered, "Allah is beautiful and loves beauty. Arrogance is to deny rights and look down upon people."[8]

Shaykh Ibn Taymiyya said that the beauty which Allah likes includes nice clothes. Hence, it could be said that Allah likes all nice things.[9] Therefore, a Muslim ought to be recognized by neat dress, cleanliness and graceful manners. Unfortunately, many Muslims lose sight of this distinction and commit errors that blemish their Muslim personality that is meant to be unique in its gracefulness, perfection and noble traits.

2.2 Cleanliness and Washing

The *sunna* is to be always clean, wearing neat dress, and smelling good. Imām Bukhārī narrated that Salmān al-Fārisī said the Prophet ﷺ said, "Allah will forgive the sins of the past week for he who on Friday takes a bath, cleanses himself, puts on his [regular] perfume or any perfume available in the house. Then, he goes out [to Friday prayer] and does not try to separate two friends. Then he prays wherever he can and listens to the Imām."[10] If the body became odorous a day or two before Friday, one should not wait until Friday to cleanse the body. We should wash our bodies as soon as it requires washing, to keep clean and fresh.

To take a bath on Friday is specifically required, as a large number of people will be gathering at the mosques. However, if our body became dirty or we perspired heavily on a particular day, then, we should take a bath at the end of the day or the next morning. This is indicated by a hadith narrated by Bukhārī and Muslim wherein Abū Hurayra reported that the Prophet ﷺ said, "It is the duty of every Muslim to have a bath [at least] once every week to wash his head and body."[11] In another hadith, the Prophet ﷺ alluded how nice it would be to remain clean, when he asked his Companions, "If one of you had a river at his door and he washed himself five times a day would any dirt remain on him?" "No dirt will remain," they answered. The Prophet ﷺ commented, "This is the example of the five [daily] prayers as Allah wipes with them your sins."[12]

Do not forget to keep with you a small bottle of perfume and to use it regularly to bring pleasure to yourself and those around you as the first hadith clearly recommends.

2.3 Arriving from a Journey

If you are travelling to visit someone, or if you are about to receive guests, make sure that your hands, feet, and socks are clean, and that your appearance and clothing are neat. Even if those in question are your parents, relatives, peers or friends of a different age, never neglect or underestimate the importance of your look, for that could certainly dull the pleasure of the meeting by marring the enjoyment of those you meet. In this regard, the Prophet ﷺ directed his Companions upon returning from a journey, saying, "You are on your way to meet your brothers, put on a nice dress and fix your saddles so you appear distinct among people as a beauty mark [on a beautiful face]. Allah does not like roughness or rough manners."

Do your best to bring some gifts to those receiving you, and likewise present your guests with a present. Always be prepared to reciprocate gifts with suitable ones. A gift, however symbolic, will greatly enhance the pleasure of such a meeting. The joy of seeing your beloved ones will be vividly remembered for many years every time your gift is seen or used. The Prophet ﷺ as reported by Bukhārī said, "Exchange gifts; exchange love." Our Muslim predecessors used to leave their host with a present that could be as symbolic as an *arak* stick.[13]

2.4 Dressing Properly

Dress neatly, even with friends and relatives. Dress properly when visiting your parents, a pious person, an elder, a relative or a friend. Your attire should be clean and elegant, not ugly or unsightly. We are attracted or repulsed by what we see, and if you look good in clean clothes, smelling nice, you will be pleasant to look at and people will be attracted to you and enjoy your presence. If you were the opposite, people will look down on you even if you were a relative or friend. To look neat while visiting or being visited is an instinctive trait in addition to being an Islamic manner. Do not ignore this aspect because you consider yourself close to your hosts or guests.

Imām Bukhārī in his book *al-Adab al-Mufrad* reported that the great *Tābiʿī*[14] [or Successor] Abū'l-ʿAliya al-Riyaḥī al-Baṣrī said,

"Muslims wore their best when visiting each other." Al-Ḥāfiẓ al-Haythamī in *Majma^c al-Zawā'id* reported that Thābit al-Banānī, the student of Imām Anas ibn Mālik, said, "When I used to visit Anas, he would call for a perfume and run it along his cheeks."[15]

Accordingly, if you were visited at home while in casual clothing, as it sometimes happens, you should change for your visitors. This will enhance their respect for you and will complement your hospitality. It is, after all, the manners of the early Muslims.

Chapter Three

ENTERING OR LEAVING A HOUSE

3.1 How to Enter

Enter or leave your house or office with your right foot first, for this was the tradition of the Prophet ﷺ. Imām Abū al-ᶜAlā Ḥasan ibn Aḥmad al-Hamazānī, a great scholar of hadith of his time, was so keen on applying this *sunna* to the extent that if someone entered his house with their left foot first, he would ask them to go out and re-enter with their right foot first. He was so much respected that the sultan of the day would visit him at school and sit in front of him as a student. At one occasion he told the sultan to exit with his right foot first and walk on the right side of the road.

When entering or leaving a house, do not push open the door violently or slam it shut, nor leave it to close by itself wildly. Such actions stand in contrast to the gracefulness of Islam to which you are honoured to belong. Close the door quietly with your hand. You may have heard a hadith reported by Muslim wherein ᶜĀ'isha, may Allah be pleased with her, quotes the Messenger of Allah ﷺ, "Gentleness adorns every act. Its absence will tarnish it."[16]

3.2 Entering While Others are Asleep

Be quiet and gentle if you enter a place where people are sleeping, whether during day or night. Be considerate. Do not cause any undue noise when entering or exiting. You have heard the saying of the Prophet ﷺ, "Whoever is deprived of gentleness is deprived of all sorts of goodness." Muslim and Tirmidhī reported that the honourable Companion al-Miqdād ibn al-Aswad said, "We used to keep for the Prophet ﷺ his share of milk, and when he would come at night he would greet us with a voice loud enough for those awake to hear, without disturbing those who were asleep."[17] In addition, whenever the Prophet ﷺ used to pray at night, he would recite the Quran with a voice that pleased those awake, without disturbing those who were asleep.

Princess Qater al-Nada was famous for her intelligence, manners and beauty. She was the daughter of Khimārawayh ibn Aḥmad ibn Tūlān,[18] the King of Egypt. She married the Abbasid Khalīfa al-Mu'tadad Billah who admired her refined manners and excellent education. Qater al-Nada said, "My father taught me an important manner: do not sleep among sitting people and do not sit among sleeping people."

3.3 Greetings

When entering or leaving your house, acknowledge those inside by using the greeting of Muslims and the motto of Islam, *As-salāmu ᶜAlaykum wa Raḥmatullāhi wa Barakātuhu* ["May the peace, mercy and blessings of Allah be upon you"]. Do not forego this Islamic greeting by saying something else such as "Good Morning" or "Hello." This greeting is the sign of Islam and the phrase that the Messenger of Allah ﷺ recommended and used. The Prophet ﷺ taught his faithful servant Anas ibn Mālik to greet his family when entering or leaving his house. Imām Tirmidhī reported that Anas said, "The Messenger of Allah ﷺ said to me, 'My son, greet your family when you enter [your home], for that is a blessing for you and your family.'"

Qatāda ibn Di'ama al-Sadūsī, a prominent *Tābiᶜī*,[19] said, "Greet your family when you enter your house. They are the most worthy of your greeting." Tirmidhī reported another hadith wherein Abū Hurayra stated that the Messenger of Allah ﷺ said, "If you join a gathering, greet them, and if you want to leave, greet them. The first is no less important than the second."[20]

Imām al-Suyūṭī in his book *Praising the Abyssinians* cited the following from the book of *al-Taḥiyāt* by Abū Ṭālib al-Jumaḥī, "Every nation has its own way of greeting. Arabs will say *salām*. Persian Emperors require prostrating and kissing the floor. The Zoroastrians touch their hand on the floor in front of the king. The Abyssinians quietly gather their hands at their chest. The Romans uncover their heads and bow. The Nubians would gesture as if kissing the guest and then put both hands on the face." All these greetings, except the *salām*, are forbidden for Muslims.

Imām Nawawī in *al-Majmūᶜ* said, "It is preferred to say *Bismillāh al-Raḥmān al-Raḥīm* ["In the name of Allah, Most Gracious, Most Merciful"] when you enter your house or the houses of others. You should say *salām* even if you enter vacant or uninhabited places and say a prayer when you go out. Tirmidhī and Abū Dāwūd narrated a hadith by Anas that the Prophet ﷺ said, "If someone says 'In the name of Allah, I seek help from Allah. There is no strength or might except with Allah,' then he will be told, 'You are protected and saved,' and Satan will leave him.""[21]

He cited another hadith narrated by Muslim that Jābir ibn ᶜAbdullāh heard the Prophet ﷺ say, "If you enter your house and pray to Allah when entering and before your meals, Satan will say [to his minions], 'No sleep and no food.' If you enter without praying to Allah, Satan will say [to his minions], 'You have got your sleep and meal.'""[22]

3.4 Announcing Your Presence

When entering a house, make your presence known to those inside before you approach them. Avoid startling or frightening them and do not descend upon them suddenly. Abū ᶜUbayda ᶜĀmir ibn ᶜAbdullāh ibn Masᶜūd said, "My father ᶜAbdullāh ibn Masᶜūd, used to announce his arrival by calling his family in a cordial tone." Imām Aḥmad ibn Ḥanbal said, "When a person enters his house, it is recommended that he makes noise by clearing his throat or tapping his shoes." His son ᶜAbdullāh said, "When returning home from the mosque, my father used to announce his arrival before entering, by tapping with his shoes or clearing his throat."

Imām Bukhārī and Muslim reported that Jābir ibn ᶜAbdullāh narrated that the Prophet ﷺ denounced those who unexpectedly surprise their families at night, whether returning from a trip or otherwise, as if they distrusted them and want to discover what goes on behind their backs.[23]

3.5 Seeking Permission to Enter

If family members are resting in their rooms and you want to join them, it is appropriate to ask for permission or to knock on the door. Otherwise, you may see them in a condition that either you or they may dislike. This applies to the entire household: immediate family or otherwise. In *al-Muwaṭṭa*, Imām Mālik narrated a hadith transmitted by ᶜAṭā' ibn Yasār that a man asked the Messenger of Allah ﷺ, "Should I seek permission to enter my mother's room?" The Prophet ﷺ answered, "Yes." The man said, "We live together in the same house." The Messenger of Allah ﷺ said, "Ask permission to join her." The man argued, "But I serve her!" The Prophet ﷺ said, "Ask for permission. Would you like to see her naked?" The man replied, "No!" The Prophet ﷺ said, "Then ask permission before entering."[24]

Similarly, a man asked ᶜAbdullāh ibn Masᶜūd, "Should I ask permission to enter my mother's room?" He answered, "Yes, there are certain circumstances in which you would rather not see her." In another narration, Zaynab, the wife of ᶜAbdullāh ibn Masᶜūd said that before opening the door of his house, ᶜAbdullāh used to make noise, lest he surprises and embarrasses his family. Likewise, a man asked Ḥudhayfa ibn al-Yamān, "Should I ask permission to enter my mother's room?" Ḥudhayfa replied, "Yes, if you do not ask for her permission, you may cause yourself a needless embarrassment."

Mūsā the son of the Companion Ṭalḥa ibn ᶜUbaydullāh said, "My father went to my mother's room. I followed him as he entered. He turned towards me and pushed me down forcing me to sit. Then he reprimanded me, 'How dare you to enter without permission?'"

Nāfiᶜ, the companion of ᶜAbdullāh ibn ᶜᶜUmar, said, "When any of the children of Ibn ᶜUmar came of age, Ibn ᶜUmar would assign that child another room. He would not allow any of them to enter his room without permission."

ᶜAṭā' ibn Abī Rabāḥ reported that he asked Ibn ᶜAbbās, "Should I seek permission when calling on my two sisters?" Ibn ᶜAbbās answered, "Yes." I said, "I am their guardian, supporter and provider of their needs." He said, "Would you rather see them naked?" Then he recited the Quranic verse, *And when the children among you come of age, let them ask for permission, as do those senior to them in age; thus does Allah make clear His signs. Allah is all-knowing, all-wise* (Quran, 24:59). Thus, Ibn ᶜAbbās concluded that seeking permission is obligatory for all people.

Ibn Masᶜūd said, "A person should seek permission whenever entering the room of a father, a mother, a brother or a sister." Jābir also said, "A person should seek permission whenever entering the room of a son, a daughter, a mother - even if she is old, a brother, a sister, or a father."

3.6 Knocking and Ringing

Knock at the door, or ring the door bell in a pleasant way and not louder than is necessary to make your presence known. Do not knock loudly and violently or ring the bell continuously. Remember that you are a visitor and not a thug or an oppressor raiding the house and frightening its occupants. A woman came to

Imām Aḥmad ibn Ḥanbal seeking his opinion on a religious matter. She banged at his door loudly. He came out saying, "This is the banging of the police." Likewise, Bukhārī reported in *al-Adab al-Mufrad* that the Companions of the Prophet ﷺ used to knock on the door of the Prophet ﷺ with the tips of their fingers.

This soft and gentle knocking, or ringing, is appropriate for those whose living quarters are close to the door. For those living farther from the door, it is appropriate to knock on their door, without banging, or ring the bell loud enough to enable them to hear it. In this regard the Prophet ﷺ said, "Gentleness adorns every act. Its absence will tarnish it." In addition, Muslim reported that the Prophet ﷺ also said, "Whoever lacks kindness, lacks all good things."

Leave an adequate time between two knocks or rings. This will enable those performing ablution, praying, or eating to finish without making them rush. Some scholars estimate this interval to be that of the praying time of four *rakʿas* [prostrations]. Keep in mind that a person may have just started the prayers just before you rang the doorbell.

After three spaced knocks, or intermittent rings, you may feel that the person you came to see is busy, otherwise he or she would have answered you. If this is the case, then leave. Bukhārī and Muslim reported that the Prophet ﷺ said, "If you sought permission three times, and were not granted permission, then you must leave."[25] While waiting for permission, do not stand in front of the door. Instead, stand to the right or to the left. The Messenger of Allah ﷺ, upon coming to someone's door, avoided facing the door directly. Instead, he would stand to the right or to the left of the door.

3.7 Identifying Oneself

If you knock on a door and are asked, "Who is it?" identify yourself by giving your common name. Do not respond with, "It is me," "Somebody," or "Guess who?" These words are useless in identifying who is at the door. You should not assume that those inside would recognize your voice, as it may resemble another person's voice. Don't forget that people differ in their ability to distinguish voices.

The Prophet ﷺ discouraged one from saying, "It's me" because it does not reveal your name. Bukhārī reported that Jābir ibn ᶜAbdullāh said, "I came to the Prophet ﷺ and knocked on his door and he asked, 'Who is it?' I answered, 'It is me.' The Prophet ﷺ disapprovingly said, 'Me is me, me is me!'"[26] For this reason, the Companions used to mention their names whenever they were asked, "Who is it?"

In another hadith, Bukhārī reported that Abū Dharr said, "One night while walking I saw the Messenger of Allah ﷺ walking by himself. I walked behind him in the shade of the moon, but he turned around and saw me and asked, "Who is there?" I replied, "It's Abū Dharr."[27] This is further confirmed by another hadith reported by Bukhārī that Umm Hānī, a cousin of the Prophet ﷺ and the sister of ᶜAlī ibn Abī Ṭālib, said, "I came to see the Prophet ﷺ. He was taking a bath and his daughter Fāṭima was holding a sheet to cover him, and he asked, "Who is this?" I replied, "I am Umm Hānī."[28]

Chapter Four

THE MANNERS OF VISITING

4.1 Keeping Appointments

In the first verse of Sūrat al-Mā'ida, Allah called upon the believers, *O you who believe! Fulfil your promises* (Quran, 5:1). Allah also praised Prophet Ismāʿīl, *He was true to his promise, He was a Messenger and a Prophet* (Quran, 19:54).

Keeping appointments is vital to our lives. Time is the most precious commodity. Once wasted, it can never be recovered. If you made an appointment, whether with a friend, colleague or for business, you should do your utmost to keep this appointment. This is the right of the other persons who, despite other commitments, favoured you with a part of their valuable time. If you do not come on time, not only have you disrupted their schedule but you have also marred your image and reputation. If your punctuality becomes poor, you will lose people's respect. You should keep all your appointments whether they are with an important person, a close friend or a business colleague. You will then be responding to the call of Allah, *And keep the promise; the promise is a responsibility* (Quran, 17:34).

It is enough to know that our kind Prophet ﷺ gave an appointment to one of his Companions. The Companion came three days later. The Prophet ﷺ gently reprimanded him saying, "You have caused me some trouble. I have been waiting for you for three days." The Companion probably had an excuse for this delay; however, he had no means by which to inform the Prophet ﷺ about his inability to keep the appointment.

Today, fast and reliable communication means are available everywhere. Therefore, as soon as you realize you will be unable to keep an appointment, you should inform the other parties to enable them to utilize their time elsewhere. Do not be careless or irresponsible assuming that since the appointment is relatively unimportant, it does not merit a notice or an apology. This is totally irrelevant. Regardless of its importance, an appointment is a commitment that should be kept or properly cancelled in advance.

Never make a promise while intending not to keep it. This is forbidden as it falls within lying and hypocrisy. Bukhārī and Muslim narrated that the Prophet ﷺ said, "Three traits single out a hypocrite, even if he prays or fasts and claims to be Muslim: If he speaks, he lies. If he makes a promise, he does not keep it. If he is entrusted, he betrays the trust."[29]

Imām al-Ghazālī in *al-Iḥyā'* explains that this hadith is applicable to those who promise while intending not to fulfil it, or those who, without excuse, decide later not to fulfil the promise. Those who promise but could not fulfil their promise due to a proper excuse are not hypocrites. But we should be careful not to present a false excuse, as Allah knows our inner thoughts and intentions.

4.2 Declining a Visit

If you visit friends with or without an appointment and they apologize for not being able to receive you, accept their apology without any ill feelings. You should understand that something might have come up compelling them to decline your visit. Their previous plans, or the state of their house, may have made your visit inconvenient. It is perfectly reasonable for them to ask to be excused. This particular etiquette is very important in order to remove any ill feelings that could linger because of declining a visit. Allah says, *If you were asked to go back, go back; that makes for greater purity* (Quran, 24:28).

Many people do not know what to do and become disturbed by the visit of someone whom they do not want to receive under the circumstances, and may resort to lying. Not only do their children learn these bad manners, but also such behaviour may lead to antipathy.

The Quranic etiquette provides a better alternative to such unpleasantness and guards us against lying. It provides for the host to kindly present a reason to the visitors and asks that they accept it in good faith and without hesitation: *If you were asked to go back, go back; that makes for greater purity* (Quran, 24:28).

The *Tābiʿī* Qatāda ibn Di'ama al-Sadūsī said, "Do not hang around the door of those who decline to receive your visit. Accept their reason, move on to attend to your business, and let them attend to theirs." Do not ask for a reason or an explanation, for Imām Mālik used to say, "Not all people can disclose their excuses." Accordingly, when it comes to visiting, our righteous forbears used to say to their hosts, "Perhaps you just became busy and cannot receive us," making them feel at ease in case they wanted to be excused. Imām al-Ṭabarī in his *Tafsīr* reported that a man of the Muhājirīn said, "All my life, I wanted to practice this verse, *If you were asked to go back, go back; that makes for greater purity* (Quran, 24:28), but I could not. I was hoping I would seek permission to visit a brother and he would tell me to 'Go back!' I would have gladly left, thus fulfilling the commandment of Allah."[30]

4.3 Control Your Eyes

When asking permission to enter a home, avoid glancing unnecessarily at its interior or beyond the guests' quarters. This is shameful and harmful. Abū Dāwūd and al-Ṭabarānī explained that Saʿd ibn ʿUbada said, "A man stood facing the door of the Prophet

ﷺ while asking permission to enter. The Prophet ﷺ said, 'Turn this way,' turning him away and ordering him to move farther from the door, saying, 'Asking permission is prescribed to prevent intrusion.'"

Bukhārī also explained in *al-Adab al-Mufrad* that the Companion Thawbān recounted that the Prophet ﷺ said, "A person should not look inside a house before getting permission. If you do [look inside before asking permission], you have already entered [that is, trespassed]." Abū Dāwūd, Tirmidhī and Bukhārī stated in *al-Adab al-Mufrad* a hadith by Abū Hurayra who said that the Messenger of Allah ﷺ said, "If the sight leaps, permission should be denied."[31] Also, Bukhārī narrated that ʿAmmār ibn Saʿīd al-Tujibī reported that ʿUmar ibn al-Khaṭṭāb said, "Whoever fills his eyes with the sight of the interior of a house before being permitted is a wrong-doer."

Bukhārī, Muslim and others narrated that Sahl ibn Saʿd said that a man peeked through a hole into the room of the Prophet ﷺ while he was scratching his head with a small pitchfork. When the Prophet ﷺ saw the intruder, he told him, "Had I known you were looking I would have poked your eye! Asking permission was prescribed to prevent intrusion."[32]

4.4 Removing Your Shoes

As a rule, you should take off your shoes unless your host asks you to keep them on. Remove your shoes at an appropriate spot, and set them in an orderly fashion. Do not forget the manner in which you put shoes on and take them off. Take off the left shoe first then the right, and then [when preparing to leave] put on the right shoe first. Imām Muslim and other scholars narrated that the Prophet ﷺ said, "When you put your shoes on, start with the right shoe. When taking your shoes off, start with the left one. The right shoe is the first to be put on and the last to be taken off." Before entering your house or that of your brethren look at your shoes. If they are dirty, remove the dirt or brush the shoes against the ground. Islam is the religion of cleanliness and courtesy.

4.5 Choosing a Seat

Sit where requested by your host. Do not argue with your host about the place they wish you to sit. If you sit where you want, you may overlook a private area of the house, or you may cause inconvenience to the house residents. Ibn Kathīr narrated in *al-Bidāya wa al-Nihāya* that when the honoured Companion ʿAdī ibn Ḥatam al-Ṭā'ī embraced Islam, he came to Madinah to see the Prophet ﷺ. The Prophet ﷺ honoured Ḥatam by motioning him to sit on a cushion, while he himself sat on the floor. ʿAdī recounts the event saying, .." then the Prophet ﷺ took me along to his house, and when we went inside, he took a leather cushion filled with palm fibre and threw it on the floor. 'Sit on this,' he said, 'No, you sit on it,' I responded. The Prophet ﷺ insisted, 'No, you.' So I sat on it while the Prophet ﷺ sat on the floor."

Kharija ibn Ziyāda visited Ibn Sīrīn and found him sitting on a cushion on the floor and wanted to sit like him, saying, "I wish to sit as you sit." Ibn Sīrīn replied, "In my home, I will not be content to provide you with my ordinary seat. Sit where you are asked to sit."

Do not sit in the host's seat unless he invites you to do so. In this regard, the Prophet ﷺ said, "No person shall lead another in prayer while at the latter's house. No person shall sit, uninvited, at the favourite seat of the master of the house."

If you arrive early to a gathering and your host, out of kindness, directed you to sit at the most prominent seat, be prepared to stand up and give this seat to the elders, the notables or the scholars when they arrive after you. They deserve this seat more than you do. Do not be insensitive and tactless. If you refuse to give your seat to those who traditionally deserve it, you only indicate your lack of manners and common sense. You will become one of those referred to by the Prophet ﷺ when he said, "Those who do not respect our elders do not belong to us."

To remain entrenched in your seat will not elevate your status, and it will certainly raise eyebrows among those present. You will be considered arrogant if you insist upon an undeserved honour. This rule applies equally to men and women. Insensibility does not enhance social status. On the contrary, it is a terrible mistake that will only tarnish one's reputation. To honour an honourable person will only improve your standing and stir admiration for your manners and humbleness.

If you sat in the second best place and a notable person entered the room, you should give your seat to that person. To be respectful of the elders testifies to your good manners and social sense. Imām Muslim reported that when organizing prayers the Prophet ﷺ said, "The wisest of you and the elders should stand behind me, then those below them, then those below them."[33]

A prominent person may call upon you to discuss a matter, or to answer a query, or to give you an advice. If you sit beside or near him, it is desirable that you return to your previous seat once the matter is concluded, unless that person or other notables insist that you remain at your new seat. Decline the invitation politely if the place will become so crowded as to cause discomfort to those already sitting there. Manners are based on common sense and could be developed by socializing with prominent and tactful individuals. By observing how they act and behave, you will be able to enhance your common sense, good manners and graceful behaviour.

You might be called to a gathering where you are the youngest. In such cases, do not sit before you are invited to do so. Do not sit if you will be crowding out others, or forcing them to leave their seats for you. If you are invited to sit, do not proceed to the best place if others deserve it and be prepared to give your seat to them. Doing this on your own, before being prompted to do so, will enhance admiration and respect for you.

4.6 A Visitor is Not an Inspector

When you enter a home, whether as a visitor or an overnight guest, do not closely examine its contents as an inspector would. Limit your observation to what you need to see. Do not open closed closets or boxes. Do not inspect a wallet, a package or a covered object. This is against Islamic manners and an impolite betrayal of the trust your host has accorded to you. Uphold these manners during your visit and seek to cultivate your host's love and respect, may Allah bless and protect you.

Imām al-Muḥāsibī in *Risālat al-Mustarshidīn* said, "The duty of sight is to preclude forbidden sights and not to try to see what has been hidden or covered. Likewise Dāwūd al-Ṭā'ī said, 'I was told we would be accountable for our minor gazes, as we are accountable for our minor deeds.'" The Arab poet, Miskīn al-Dārimī said, "My neighbour need not worry if his door is not closed."

4.7 Burdening Hosts with Requests

Whether visiting friends or relatives, one must avoid unnecessary requests that may cause inconvenience to the hosts. For example, avoid using their phone, going to the toilet, or performing your ablution. Good manners dictate that you should be considerate, for not every house may have these facilities prepared for the convenient use of its guests. Its condition or location could be embarrassing for your hosts. Prepare yourself in the convenience of your home before paying visits. Your hosts will be very pleased if your visit was free of inconvenience and embarrassment.

4.8 Timing Your Visit

Choose an appropriate time for your visit. Do not visit at inconvenient times, such as meal-time or when people are sleeping, resting or relaxing. The length of the visit should correspond with how well you know the hosts, as well as their circumstances and conditions. Do not overstay your welcome by making your visit too long or burdensome. Imām al-Nawawī said, "It is strongly recommended for Muslims to visit the pious people, their brethren, neighbours, friends and relatives, and to be generous, kind and obliging to them. However, the extent of the visit varies according to the host's circumstances. The visit ought to be conducted in a pleasant manner and at convenient times. There are numerous sayings and traditions in this regard."[34]

4.9 Greeting a Group

If you enter a room, greet everyone inside. If you want to shake hands with those present, start with the most prominent, the most knowledgeable, the most pious, the oldest or those who have similar Islamic distinctions. Do not start with the first person you see on your right; you may overlook the most distinguished or most prominent. If you cannot decide who is that person, or if those present happen to be of comparable status, then start with the elderly, for they are easier to recognize. Bukhārī explained that the Prophet ﷺ said, "The elder! The elder!"[35] In another version he said, "The elders come first." Abū Yaʿla and al-Ṭabarānī in *al-Awsaṭ* reported that the Prophet ﷺ said, "Start with the elders," or, he said, "Start with the notables."

4.10 Sitting Between Two People

If you enter a room, do not sit between two people. Instead, sit on their left or right. Abū Dāwūd reported that the Messenger of Allah ﷺ said, "No one is to sit between two people without their permission."[36]

Sometimes the two persons will be kind enough to favour you by making room for you to sit between them. Acknowledge this kind gesture by thankfully accepting their offer. Be grateful and good mannered, do not sit cross-legged to crowd them out. A sage once said, "Two people are truly ungrateful: a person to whom you give advice and he hates you for it, and a person who is favoured with a seat in a tight place and he sits cross-legged."[37]

If you are seated next to two people, do not eavesdrop and listen to what they say, for it could be that their conversation be a confidential or a private matter. Eavesdropping is a bad habit and a sin. Bukhārī reported that the Messenger of Allah ﷺ said, "Whoever listens to people's conversation against their wishes will be punished by liquid lead being poured down their ears on the Day of Judgment."[38]

You should seek to benefit from the company and wisdom of the elders who traditionally are described as "A fruit at the end of the season." And I would add to that, "A sun setting among the clouds." Soon they will depart leaving us behind. Be keen to attend the gatherings of the elders, whether scholars, pious persons, nobles or relatives. Soon you may lament their departure and your irrecoverable loss.

It is an inappropriate manner to whisper to someone sitting next to you if you are in a group of three. The third person will feel isolated and will harbour the worst of thoughts. The Messenger of Allah ﷺ disapproved of this. Imām Mālik and Abū Dāwūd reported that the Prophet ﷺ said, "No two shall exchange whispers in the presence of a third person."[39] The Prophet ﷺ said "No two..." in an assertive negative form, indicating that such a mistake is not only inappropriate but despicable. Another hadith in Bukhārī says, "If you were three, two of you should not whisper to each other till you join other people, lest the third feel offended."[40] ʿAbdullāh ibn ʿUmar was asked, "What if they were four?" "Then it does not matter," he answered; meaning it would not be then offensive. Whispers are usually secrets, so if a friend entrusted you with a secret, do not betray it. Do not tell it even to your best friend or closest relative.

4.11 The Duties of the Host and the Rights of the Guest

If you are having a guest overnight, be hospitable and generous. But do not exaggerate when providing food and drink to your guest. Moderation, not excess, is the *sunna*. You should try your best to make your guest's stay pleasant and comfortable during the day and night. Inform your guest of the direction of *qibla* and show them the way to the bathroom.

Your guest will need to use towels after ablution, having a shower or washing hands before and after meals. Make sure that these are fresh and clean. Do not offer towels that you or family members have used. It is also a nice idea to provide the guest with perfume and a mirror. Make sure the toiletries and bath accessories they will be using are clean and sanitized. Before leading your guest to the bathroom, inspect it and remove anything you don't want your guest to see.

Your guests will need rest and a quiet sleep. Spare them the noise of the children and the house as much as possible. Remove intimate clothing from their view. If the guest is a man, remove all women's clothing and belongings. This is a desirable and decent practice that will leave you both feeling comfortable. When meeting your guests, receive them with tact and respect. Dress properly and look your best but do not overdo it. The close relationship between you is no excuse for negligence or indecency in your manner or appearance. Imām Bukhārī in *al-Adab al-Mufrad* reported that our forefathers used to look their best when visiting each other. Be kind and considerate with your guests. As a rule, do not ask them to help you with house chores. Imām al-Shāfiʿī said, "Gentlemen do not employ their visiting guests."

If you visit a relative or a friend, you should be mindful of your host's circumstances and work commitments. Make your visit as brief as possible, as everybody has various jobs and duties. Be considerate of your hosts and volunteer to help them with their business, house chores and obligations. While at your host's house, do not inspect and examine every corner, especially when you are invited beyond the guest room, lest you see something you're not supposed to notice. In addition, do not bother your hosts by being inquisitive and asking too many questions whether about themselves, their household or the house itself.

4.12 Stay in Touch

If you could not visit your relatives, friends or acquaintance, you could still keep in touch by calling them or sending them a letter. This will leave them with a deep amicable impression, and will keep the relationship alive. Al-Faḍl ibn Marwān, the vizier of the Abbasid Khalīfa al-Muᶜtaṣim, said, "Inquiring about friends is [like] meeting them." In this regard, I would like to quote two poems:

> If dear friends missed meeting each other
> Then, the best meeting is a letter

> I will be grateful everyday
> To a friend sending greetings while far away

4.13 Brief Advice to My Sisters

I would like to give a special advice to my dear Muslim sisters. If you want to visit your relatives or your Muslim sisters, carefully select the day and the hour of your visit and its duration. There are appropriate and inappropriate times for paying visits even to relatives and friends.

Do your best to make the visit a nice, brief, and pleasant one. Avoid turning it into a boring, wearisome, inquisitive and lengthy visit. Instead, it should be a visit whose purpose is to rekindle and nourish an old friendship or kinship. The visit is desirable if it is short and considerate, and it is undesirable if it is long and tedious during which conversation moves from being purposeful and valuable to being aimless and trivial. The honourable *Tābiᶜī* Muḥammad ibn Shihāb al-Zuhrī said, "When a meeting becomes too long, Satan increasingly participates in it."

During the visit, make sure that most if not all of your talk is of value and benefit. Keep away from backbiting, gossips and idle talk. Astute Muslim women do not have time for such nonsense.

Chapter Five

THE MANNERS OF CONVERSATION

5.1 Selecting Suitable Topics

In the Sūrat al-Ḥajj, Allah described the believers, *And they have been guided to the purest of talk; and guided to the path of Him who is worthy of all praise* (Quran, 22:24). When you talk during your visit, say only what befits the situation and be brief. If you are the youngest among those present, don't speak unless you are asked to, or unless you know that your talk will be well received and will please the host and the other guests. Don't prolong your speech; your talk should be clear, concise and to the point. Do not talk on and on. Bukhārī reported that Anas said, "The Prophet's ﷺ speech was clear and succinct, neither too long nor too short, and he disliked chattering and ranting."[41] Similarly Bukhārī and Muslim narrated a hadith in which ʿĀ'isha said, "The Prophet ﷺ spoke [so few words] that you could count his words."[42]

If you hear the *adhān,* stop talking, listen to it and respond to the call of Allah. Many people, even those with Islamic knowledge, continue talking while the *adhān* is being called. This is rude, as those hearing the *adhān* should listen to it and quit speech, study and even the recitation of the Quran. Thoughtfully, they should repeat the words of the *adhān* and reflect on the meaning of this heavenly call.

We should listen to the *adhān*, whether we are at home, in the office or attending a lesson—even a religious one. The great Ḥanafī Imām al-Kasānī in *Badai'u al-Sana'ī* said, "Those hearing the *adhān* or *iqāma* should not talk. Everything should be stopped in order to listen and respond to the *adhān*; even reading the Quran or other noble things [should cease]."[43]

The *adhān* nourishes the Muslim soul with faith and nearness to Allah, so do not forego your share of it; and teach this to your children and friends. Abū Saʿīd al-Khudrī narrated that the Prophet ﷺ said, "If you hear the *adhān*, repeat what the *mu'adhdhin* is saying."[44] In another hadith reported by Jābir, the Prophet ﷺ said, "He deserves my help on the Day of Judgment who says when hearing *adhān*, 'O Allah, the Lord of this perfect call and imminent prayer, please award Muḥammad the help, virtues and the desired status you promised him.'"[45]

Imām ʿAbd al-Razzāq narrated in his *Musannaf* that Ibn Jurayj said, "I was told that people used to listen to the *adhān* in the same manner they would listen to recitation of Quran. They would repeat after the *mu'adhdhin*. If he said, 'Come to prayer,' they would respond, 'With the help and power of Allah.' If he said, 'Come to success,' they would say, 'With the will of Allah.'"[46]

5.2 Talk in a Suitable Tone

If you speak to a guest or any other person, whether in a gathering or alone, make sure that your voice is pleasant, with a low but audible tone. Raising your voice is contrary to proper manners and indicates a lack of respect for the person to whom you are talking. This manner should be maintained with friends, peers, acquaintances, strangers, the young and the old. It is more important to adhere to this with one's parents or someone of their status, or with people for whom you have great respect. If appropriate, smile while talking to others. This will make them more receptive to what you have to say, and may dispel the impression that observant Muslims are stern and humourless.

The Quran relates to us the advice of Luqmān the sage to his son, *"And lower your voice"* (Quran, 31:19), directing him to speak in a gentle manner, for speaking loudly is detested and ugly. Likewise, verses two and three of Sūrat al-Ḥujurāt read, *O you who believe! Raise not your voices above the voice of the Prophet, nor speak aloud to him as you speak aloud to one another, lest your deeds become vain and you perceive not. Those that lower their voices in the presence of Allah's apostle, Allah has tested their hearts for piety, for them there is forgiveness and a great reward* (Quran, 44:2-3).

Imām Bukhārī reported that ᶜAbdullāh ibn al-Zubayr said that after the revelation of this verse, whenever ᶜUmar ibn al-Khaṭṭāb wanted to speak to the Prophet ﷺ, he would talk almost in whispers and the Prophet ﷺ could hardly hear him and would ask him to repeat what he said.[47]

Al-Ḥāfiẓ al-Dhahabī wrote in his biography of Imām Ibn Sīrīn, the great scholar and eminent *Tābiᶜī*, "Whenever he was in his mother's presence, he would talk in such a hushed voice that you would think he was ill."[48] In his biography of ᶜAbdullāh ibn ᶜAwn al-Baṣrī, a student of Imām Ibn Sīrīn and one of the famous scholars, al-Ḥāfiẓ al-Dhahabī noted, "One time his mother called him and because he responded with a voice louder than hers, he was fearful and repentant, thus freeing two slaves."[49] ᶜĀṣim ibn Bahdilah al-Kūfī, the reciter of the Quran, said, "I visited ᶜUmar ibn ᶜAbd al-ᶜAzīz, and a man spoke very loudly, and ᶜUmar replied, "Stop it. You need not talk that loud. Talk loud enough only to make your listeners hear.""[50]

5.3 The Art of Listening

If a person starts telling you, whether you are alone or in the company of others, something that you already knew very well, you should pretend as if you do not know it. Do not rush to reveal your knowledge or to interfere with the speech. Instead, show your attention and concentration. The honourable *Tābiᶜī* Imām ᶜAṭā ibn Abī Rabāḥ said, "A young man would tell me something that I may have heard before he was born. Nevertheless, I listen to him as if I had never heard it before."

Khālid ibn Ṣafwān al-Tamīmī, who frequented the courts of two Khalīfas; ʿUmar ibn ʿAbd al-ʿAzīz and Hisham ibn ʿAbd al-Mālik, said, "If a person tells you something you have heard before, or news that you already learnt, do not interrupt him to exhibit your knowledge to those present. This is rude and ill-mannered." The honourable Imām ʿAbdullāh ibn Wahab al-Qurashī al-Maṣrī, a companion of Imām Mālik, al-Layth ibn Saʿd and al-Thawrī, said, "Sometimes a person would tell me a story that I have heard before his parents had wed. Yet I listened as if I have never heard it before." Ibrāhīm ibn al-Junayd said, "A wise man said to his son, 'Learn the art of listening as you learn the art of speaking.'" Listening well means maintaining eye contact, allowing the speaker to finish the speech and restraining your urge to interrupt his speech. Al-Ḥāfiẓ al-Khaṭīb al-Baghdādī said in a poem:

Never interrupt a talk
Though you know it inside out

5.4 Discussions and Debates

If you have trouble understanding some of what has been said in a meeting, hold your questions until the speaker has finished. Gently, politely and with proper introduction ask for clarification. Do not interrupt a person's speech. Never raise your voice with the question, or be blunt to draw attention to yourself. This is contrary to the proper manner of listening, and it stirs up contempt. However, this is not the rule if the meeting is for study and learning. In such a case, asking questions and initiating a discussion is desirable if conducted respectfully and tactfully and only after the speaker finishes. The Khalīfa al-Ma'mūn said, "Discussion entrenches knowledge much more than mere agreement." Al-Haytham ibn ʿAdī, a known scholar, historian and a member of the court of four Caliphs—Abū Jaʿfar al-Manṣūr, al-

Mahdī, al-Hādī and al-Rashīd—said, "It is ill-mannered to overwhelm someone while speaking and to interrupt him before he ends his talk."

If a colleague did not understand an issue and asked a scholar or an elder to explain, you should listen to what is being said. The repeated explanation may give you additional insights to what you already know. Never utter any word belittling your colleague, nor allow your face to betray such attitude.

When an elder or a scholar speaks, listen attentively. Never busy yourself with a talk or discussion with other colleagues. Do not let your mind wander elsewhere, keep it focused on what is being said.

Never interrupt a speaker. Never rush to answer if you are not very confident of your answer. Never argue about something you do not know. Never argue for the sake of argument. Never show arrogance with your counterparts especially if they hold a different opinion. Do not switch the argument to belittle your opponent's views. If their misunderstanding becomes evident, do not rebuke or scold them. Be modest and kind. A poet once said:

> Who could get me a friend
> Who if I offend will remain calm
> Who would listen intently to what I have to say
> When he knows it better than I do.

5.5 Swearing by Allah

To confirm or emphasize a statement, many resort to swearing by the name of Allah or one of His attributes. This is a bad habit that should be resisted. The name of Allah should not be used so casually, and to swear by it is a very serious matter. Allah says in Sūrat al-Naḥl, *And do not take your oath to practice deception between yourselves, with the result that someone's foot may slip after it was firmly planted* (Quran, 16:94). Always remember the hadith of the Prophet ﷺ reported by Bukhārī and Muslim, "Whoever believes in Allah and the Last Day should say something good or remain silent."[51]

5.6 Answering a Question

If a colleague was asked about something that you know, do not rush to answer. Instead, you should not say anything until you are asked. This is a better manner and a nobler attitude. It generates interest in what you say, while enhancing your respect.

The honourable *Tābiʿī* Mujāhid ibn Jabr recalled that Luqmān the Wise said to his son, "If another person was asked a question, never hasten to give the answer, as if you are going to gain booty or to win a precious prize. By doing so, you will belittle the questioner, will offend the questioned and will join obnoxious people with your stupidity and ill-manners."

Shaykh Ibn Baṭṭa, a Ḥanbalī scholar, said, "I was with Abū ʿUmar al-Zāhid, Muḥammad ibn ʿAbd al-Wāḥid al-Baghdādī—the Imām and linguist known also as Ghulām Thaʿlab. He was asked about an issue. As I rushed and answered it, he turned to me and asked, 'Do you recognize an obtrusive character?' Alluding that I was a nosy person, making me feel very embarrassed."

5.7 Talking on the Phone

Keep the following basic manners in mind when making phone calls. Identify yourself by saying your full name unless you are calling someone very close to you. Do not engage in conversation or answer questions until you know who is calling. Choose the right time for your call, whether calling relatives, friends, employees or officials. Make your conversation brief and to the point, so it will not interfere with their business, or other calls they themselves have to make or receive.

Chapter Six

SOCIAL MANNERS

6.1 Respect and Favour the Elders

Recognise the status of the elders and give them due respect. When walking with them, walk slightly behind and to their right. Let them enter and exit first, open doors for them and hold it until they enter. If you meet them, greet them properly and respectfully. If you discuss something with them, let them speak first and listen attentively and graciously. If your opinion differs, you should remain polite, calm and kind-hearted, and you should lower your voice. Never forget to remain respectful.

Let me review with you some of the Prophetic sayings and traditions that uphold these polite manners. Imām Bukhārī and Muslim reported that ʿAbdullāh ibn Sahl made a trip with Mahisa ibn Masʿūd ibn Zayd to Khaybar. When they were about to return, Mahisa found ʿAbdullāh had been murdered. He went to the Prophet ﷺ with his older brother, Huwaisa and the victim's brother, ʿAbd al-Raḥmān ibn Sahl. Mahisa who witnessed the incident started to talk, but the Prophet ﷺ said, "The elder, the elder." At that, Huwaisa spoke and after him spoke Mahisa.[52] Another story further emphasizes this behaviour. When he was young, ʿAbdullāh ibn ʿUmar was at a gathering of the Prophet ﷺ and his senior Companions, like Abū Bakr and his father. The Prophet ﷺ asked his Companions, "Tell me which tree does not shed its leaves and is like the Muslim." The Companions started suggesting names of desert trees. ʿAbdullāh ibn ʿUmar thought it was the palm tree. Since he was the youngest, and seeing Abū Bakr and ʿUmar silent, he shied away and said nothing. The Prophet ﷺ told his Companions, "It is the palm tree." Later, ʿAbdullāh told his father that he knew the right answer but shied away. ʿUmar said to his son, "For you to have said it right then would have been worth a lot to me."

Imām Aḥmad and Tirmidhī reported that ʿUbāda ibn al-Samit stated that the Messenger of Allah ﷺ said, "Whoever does not respect our elders is not one of us." Another version reported, "Whoever does not respect our elders, does not show compassion to our youth and does not honour our scholars, he is not one of us."[53]

This should not be taken to belittle the youth or put them down. Imām Bukhārī reported that Ibn ʿAbbās narrated that ʿUmar allowed him to attend his council with seniors who attended the Battle of Badr. Some of them felt uneasy and asked, "Why are you permitting him to attend when he is as young as our children?" ʿUmar replied, "He is [knowledgeable], as you well know." Another version elaborates that ʿUmar asked the seniors to explain Sūrat al-Fātiḥa and only ʿAbdullāh ibn ʿAbbās explained it correctly. Ibn ʿAbbās said, "I thought he asked the question just to demonstrate my knowledge to them."[54]

6.2 Walking with the Elders

The proper manner of walking with elders was laid-out by Imām Abū Yaʿla al-Ḥanbalī; a jurist, a judge and the chief Shaykh of the Ḥanbalī school of *fiqh* of his time. His student, the jurist ʿAlī ibn Mubārak al-Karkhī said, "One day, Judge Abū Yaʿla said to me, while walking with him, 'If you walked with someone you honour, where would you walk?' I said, 'I do not know.' He said, 'Walk to his right. Place him at the position of the Imām in the prayer. Leave his left side clear in case he needs to spit or to get rid of dirt.'"[55]

An interesting story in this regard involved three Muslim scholars of the third century of the Hijra. Judge Aḥmad ibn ʿUmar ibn Surayh, Jurist Muḥammad ibn Dāwūd al-Ẓāhirī and Linguist Naftawayh were walking together when they came to a very narrow passageway. Each wanted the other to go ahead. Ibn Surayh said, "A narrow street invites ill manners." Ibn Dāwūd responded, "Though it points out status." Naftawayh said, "When friendship prevails, formalities disappear."

The story does not tell who went ahead of the others, but it is likely that it was Aḥmad ibn Surayh as he, at the time, was a judge and a prominent Imām who ranked above his two companions. He commented that, "A narrow street invites ill manners," apologizing out of politeness for going ahead. He would not have said that if one of his companions had moved ahead as that would have been impolite. However, there is a possibility that Naftawayh went ahead as his words could also be an apology for doing that, as he is the least ranked. More importantly, it is wonderful to see such considerate behaviour and tactful apologies.

6.3 The Elders Are to Lead Prayers

The Messenger of Allah ﷺ taught the youth the manners of companionship and the custom of giving precedence to elders. Bukhārī and Muslim reported that the honoured Companion Mālik ibn al-Ḥuwayrith said, "I was with a group of youth that visited the Messenger of Allah ﷺ in Madinah for twenty nights. The Messenger of Allah ﷺ was very kind and compassionate. He sensed that we might have missed our families and were homesick, and asked us about whom we had left behind. When we informed him, he said, 'Go back to your families, live with them, teach them Islam and tell them of the good deeds. At the times of prayer, let one of you call the *adhān*, and have your eldest lead the prayer.'"[56]

In this particular case, the Prophet ﷺ specified that the eldest should lead the prayers, since they were equal in their knowledge and learning. Being older in such a case merits leadership in the prayers. However, if a person is more knowledgeable, then he should lead the prayer, as knowledge is an honour above age as supported by many hadiths on this subject.

If the prayers are offered at a house, the host is entitled to lead it. Out of respect, he may invite a person who is more knowledgeable, older or more prominent. If the guest declines, the host should not hesitate to lead the prayers. Imām Aḥmad reported in his *Musnad* that ʿAbdullāh ibn Masʿūd visited Abū Mūsā al-Ashʿarī. When it was time to pray, Abū Mūsā asked Ibn Masʿūd, "Please lead the prayers as you are older and have more knowledge." Ibn Masʿūd said, "No, you lead the prayer. This is your house and praying area. You should lead the prayer." Abū Mūsā then led the prayer.[57]

6.4 The Elders Served First

When serving food or drink, give precedence to the elders or to dignitaries, ahead of anyone else. After that, you may proceed with those on their right if you want to follow the practice of the Prophet ﷺ. The evidence supporting this manner, in addition to the two hadiths mentioned earlier, is found in many hadiths, some of which are cited below.

Imām Muslim reported the following hadith in his *Ṣaḥīḥ* in the chapter on the "Manners and Rules" of eating and drinking. Ḥudhayfa ibn al-Yamān said, "Whenever we were invited to a meal with the Messenger of Allah ﷺ, we would not reach for the food with our hands before he had reached for it."

Imām al-Nawawī, in *Riyāḍ al-Ṣāliḥīn*, devoted a chapter to respecting scholars, the elders and the dignitaries; giving them precedence and the best seat and acknowledging their pre-eminence.[58] Al-Nawawī quoted the Quran and a large collection of hadith. In the following paragraphs, I will quote some of these.

Allah said in the Quran, *Are they equal, those who have knowledge and those who have no knowledge? It is those who possess understanding that receive admonition* (Quran, 39:9).

Imām Muslim reported that ʿUqba ibn ʿAmr al-Badrī al-Anṣārī stated that the Prophet ﷺ said, "Those who are best at reciting the Quran should lead prayers. If they are equal, then those most versed in the *sunna* should lead; if they are equal, then a person who migrated first [from Makkah to Madinah] should lead; if they had migrated at the same time, then an elder should lead."

Imām Muslim reported that Ibn Masʿūd said that the Prophet ﷺ said, "Let your wise and mature pray immediately behind me, then those who trail behind them, and then those who trail behind them." [59]

Imām Bukhārī reported that Jābir ibn ʿAbdullāh said, "After the Battle of Uḥud, the Prophet ﷺ buried two martyrs in one grave. He asked, 'Which one memorized more of the Quran?' When informed, he placed him first facing the *qibla*."

Muslim reported that ʿAbdullāh ibn ʿUmar stated that the Prophet ﷺ said, "I dreamt I was brushing my teeth with a *siwāk* [tree branch] when two men approached me. I handed the *siwāk* to the younger but was instructed to hand it to the older. Accordingly, I handed it to the older."

Imām Abū Dāwūd reported as a sound hadith that Abū Mūsā al-Ashʿarī stated that the Prophet ﷺ said, "Part of paying homage to Allah is to respect an elder whose hair has turned grey, a [regular] reciter of the Quran[60] or a just ruler."

This desired behaviour towards elders is so important that the Prophet ﷺ made it part of respecting and venerating Allah. To ignore this would be a gross misbehaviour. At its forefront comes respect and reverence of the just ruler. A poet listed eight points and suggested that those who implement them should be slapped on the neck: Disrespecting a grand ruler; entering a house without being invited in; giving orders at another's house; taking an undeserved seat of honour; talking to those who are not interested in what one has to say; interrupting two people while they are speaking to each other; asking charity from a miser; seeking a favour from an enemy.

Abū Dāwūd and al-Ḥākim reported as an authentic hadith that Maymūn ibn Abū Shabīb recounted that a beggar stopped the Prophet's ﷺ wife ʿĀ'isha and she gave him a piece of dry bread. At another time, a properly dressed, well-groomed man asked her for food. She let him sit and offered him a meal. When asked about that, she replied that the Prophet ﷺ said, "Treat people according to their status."

Imām al-Nawawī concluded by citing a hadith reported by Bukhārī and Muslim in which Samūra ibn Jundub said, "Though I was a young child at the time of the Prophet ﷺ, I used to listen to what he said and memorize it. Nothing prevents me from narrating my knowledge except the presence of older men."

In conclusion, the *sunna* of serving at a gathering is to start according to the following order of merits; age, knowledge, social status, lineage, veterans of *Jihād*, generosity or similar virtues. Furthermore, the *sunna* of hospitality is to start with the most prominent, then to move to those on the right of that person in order to harmonize the custom of starting on the right with the custom of starting with people of virtue.

Some people who misunderstand the real meaning of some texts of the *sunna* claim that the *sunna* is to start with those on your right whoever they are. They base this on hadiths that stress starting from the right. This is only true when those present are equal in character, status or age. However, if one of them is distinguished with a merit such as old age, then the *sunna* is to start with that person.

In his book *al-Bayān wa Taḥṣīl*, Imām Ibn Rushd said, "As a rule, if the status of those present is equal, one should start on the right, as with every desirable act. However, if a scholar, an honourable person or an elder is present, the *sunna* is to serve that person and then move to his right in a counter-clockwise fashion. The Messenger of Allah ﷺ was offered milk mixed with water while a Bedouin was sitting on his right, and to his left was sitting Abū Bakr. The Prophet ﷺ drank some and handed it over to the Bedouin saying, "From the right, then to the right."[61]

Once you have served the most prominent person, do not proceed to your right in a clockwise fashion, even if the people to your right are of higher status, unless those on the right give up their turn. The Messenger of Allah ﷺ was sitting with elders on his left and a young man on his right. He was given a drink. After drinking, he asked the young man, "Would you allow me to pass it to them?" The young man answered, "By Allah! No. I would not favour anyone with my share of your drink." The Prophet ﷺ willingly put the drink in the hand of the young man indicating that it was his right.

The Indian scholar, al-Mubārakpūrī, in his treatise on explaining *Jāmiᶜ Tirmidhī* elaborated on this issue when commenting on the hadith narrated by Ibn ᶜAbbās, "The server should be the last one to drink." Al-Mubārakpūrī said, "This indicates that the server should delay his drink until all guests have been served. The same applies when fruits are being served. The most notable should be served first, and then those on his right until everyone is served."[62]

Imām al-Mināwī commented on the previous hadith of Ibn ᶜAbbās, "This implies that the *sunna* is to continue serving drink and food with those on the right of the most noble person even if that person happened to be less important than the person on the left."[63] A hadith in *Ṣaḥīḥ Muslim* further reinforces this rule of serving the elders or most noble first and then those on his right. ᶜAbdullāh ibn Busr said, "The Prophet ﷺ visited my father and we served him a mix of dates and butter. Then he was given dates. He ate it and threw the pit using his middle and forefingers.

Then he was given a drink from which he drank and passed it to his right."[64] The words "he was given a drink" clearly indicates that he was served first, for he was the most noble person present. Likewise, it is evident he then passed it to those on his right. It indicates that the hosts started with the Prophet ﷺ out of respect and not because he asked for a drink. The preceding words "he was given dates" reinforces this understanding. It is very unlikely that the Prophet ﷺ, while a guest, will ask his host for food and then for drink. Though it could be argued that this is a possibility. It is a hypothetical possibility that lacks evidence or probability.

An important aspect of proper manners is that people extend help and hospitality to strangers out of duty and pure humanity. However, some will go an extra step in their generosity and offer more help once they learn that the person needing help has additional virtues, such as being a scholar or a notable person. This is undoubtedly evidence of a righteous attitude and strong faith that motivated such gestures.

In conclusion, the general rule is to start from the right if those present are equal in merit. However, if there was a person who is well known for a respectable trait, then start with that person.

If we were to follow the alleged rule that hosts ought to start with the person who happened to be on their right, then we could start with a young child, a servant, a driver, or a guard, and thus neglecting more prominent guests, such as a dignitary, a revered scholar, a notable, a parent, a grandparent or an uncle. Would it be acceptable by the *Sharīʿa* and its refined manners to forsake honouring people of character? We may serve ten people or more sitting on the right side before we reach the most honourable person. To serve him at the end does not befit his status and may offend him. Islamic manners definitely disapprove of this abnormal conduct.

However, if someone asks for a drink, they have the right to it before everyone else regardless of age or status, and the round should proceed with those on their right. If this person notices someone older or of higher status showing desire for the drink, he or she may willingly give up his or her right in favour of that person. When preferring others to yourself, you practice the Islamic manner of unselfishness, and you will achieve great virtue and honour and gain multiple rewards.

6.5 The Story of Qays ibn ʿĀṣim al-Tamīmī

To respect, obey and give precedence to the elders is an old established Arab and Muslim tradition. Here I would like to quote in full the advice the great Companion Qays ibn ʿĀṣim al-Tamīmī. On his deathbed, Qays advised his children to consider their elders as their leaders from whom they will receive valuable advice and sound wisdom.

Qays ibn ʿĀṣim al-Minqirī al-Tamīmī was the chieftain of the tribe of Tamīm. Famous for his eloquent speeches and wisdom, the Prophet ﷺ honoured him with the title "Master of the desert dwellers." He was a wise and mild-mannered person. In the 9th year of *al-Hijrah*, he came to visit the Prophet ﷺ in Madinah with a delegation of his tribe. When the Prophet ﷺ saw him he said, "This is the master of the desert dwellers." He lived an honourable life spending his last years in Basra, where he died in the year 20 AH.

He was known for patience and leniency. Al-Aḥnaf ibn Qays, a famous Arab sage, was once asked, "Who taught you patience and leniency?" He answered, "Qays ibn ʿĀṣim al-Minqirī. Once I saw him sitting in his courtyard talking to his guests and fellow tribesmen. A man tied-up in ropes and a dead body were brought to him. He was told, "We caught your nephew after he killed your son." Qays ibn ʿĀṣim remained calm and completed his talk. Turning to his nephew, he said, 'You have done the worst. You have sinned against your Lord; you harmed your relative and murdered your cousin. You killed yourself and weakened your tribe.'

He called another son and said to him, 'My son, untie your cousin and set him free, bury your brother, and go to his mother and give her a hundred camels to compensate her for the loss of her son.'"

Ḥasan al-Baṣrī, who met him and studied at his hands, relates that when Qays ibn ᶜĀṣim was dying, he called his thirty-three children, and advised them as follows:

> O my sons, fear Allah and remember what I will say, for no one will give you more sincere advice. When I die, make your seniors your leaders; do not make your juniors your leaders, for if you promote your seniors you will maintain your father's legacy. Do not make your juniors your leaders, for if you do so, people will not only disrespect your seniors, but will look down at you. Do not wail after my death, for I heard the Prophet ﷺ forbade wailing. Look after your wealth for it enlightens the generous and averts miserliness. Do not beg people, for that is the worst way of becoming wealthy. Avoid bad traits, it may please you once, but will displease you many times.

Qays then called for his quiver, and asked his eldest son, ᶜAlī, to take out a single arrow and break it, and he did that. He asked him to break two arrows and that he did. He then asked his son to bundle thirty arrows with a tie and break them all, but his son could not. He said, "My sons, you will be strong if united and weak if separated." Then he composed the following poem:

> Glory is what the earnest father built and the children maintained
> Glory, bravery and leniency are best adorned with chastity and generosity
> Thirty you are my sons, in face of calamities and trouble
> You are like thirty arrows bundled with a strong tie
> It will not be broken, but once separated will easily be broken
> Your elders, your best mannered, should be your leaders
> Your young should be protected and nurtured until your youngest matures

6.6 Manners with Parents

Observe full respect and reverence to your father and mother, for they are the most worthy of your consideration. Bukhārī and Muslim reported that a man asked the Prophet ﷺ, "O Messenger of Allah, who is most worthy of my best behaviour?" The Prophet ﷺ answered, "Your mother! Your mother! Your mother! Then your father, then the closer, and the closer among your relatives." Bukhārī in *al-Adab al-Mufrad* and ᶜAbd al-Razzāq in his *Musannaf* (the wording is his) reported that Hishām ibn Urwa recounted that his father told him that Abū Hurayra saw a man walking ahead of another. He asked him, "Is this man related to you?" "He is my father," the man replied. Abū Hurayra told him, "Do not walk ahead of him, do not sit until he sits and do not call him by his name."[65] According to Ibn Wahab, a student of Imām Mālik named Imām ᶜAbd al-Raḥmān ibn al-Qāsim al-ᶜUtaqī al-Maṣrī, said, "While Imām Mālik was reading *al-Muwaṭṭa* to me he suddenly stood up and left me for a long while. Then he came back and sat down. He was asked why he acted as such, and he answered, 'My mother came down asking me something. Since she was standing I stood up respectfully, when she went, I sat back down.'"

Likewise, the revered *Tābiᶜī* Ṭawūs ibn Kisān said, "It is part of the *sunna* to respect four people: a scholar, an elder, a leader, and a father. It is considered rude that a man call his father by his name." More so, at the end of his book of Mālikī *Fiqh al-Kāfī*, Imām Ibn ᶜAbd al-Barr said:

> Kindness to the parents is an obligatory duty, and by the grace of Allah, it is not so difficult. Kindness means to be humble with them, to speak to them nicely, to look at them with love and respect, to speak in a mild tone that does not surpass theirs unless they are hard of hearing, to give them complete access to your own wealth and to offer them the best of your food and drink.

Children should not walk ahead of their parents, nor speak before them in matters that they know are their fathers'. Children should wholeheartedly avoid upsetting their parents and should please them as much as possible. Making your parents' life enjoyable is one of the most virtuous acts. Children must hasten to respond to their parents' call. If a child is performing voluntary prayers, the prayer should be shortened to respond promptly. Children should only say good words to their parents.

In return, it is the parents' duty to make it easier for their children by being kind and supportive of them, for only with Allah's help are people able to obey Him and heed His commands."

You may have to go out of your way to serve your mother and father, but do not forget that their rights are beyond such difficulties. For this Allah says: *Your Lord has decreed that you worship none but Him, and that you be kind to your parents. Whether one or both of them attain old age in the life, say not a word of contempt, nor rebuff them but address them in terms of honour. And out of kindness lower to them the wing of humility, and say, "My Lord bestow mercy on them as they cherished me in childhood"* (Quran, 17:23-24). The Prophet ﷺ said, "No child will compensate a parent unless he finds him or her a slave and he frees him or her."[66]

Keep in mind that it is human nature to like to be the best in status, prestige and popularity, and to dislike that someone be better than oneself. Only your parents would wish that you become better than what they are. How should you treat those who prefer you to themselves and truly wish you the best?

6.7 Telling Your Family of Your Whereabouts

If you leave home to a place other than your usual work, it is advisable to inform your family of your whereabouts. Knowing where you keeps their mind at ease. The great *Tābiʿī* Qatāda ibn Di'ama al-Sadūsī disapproved of one going out without telling his family of his whereabouts. In this regard, Imām Aḥmad reported that Qatāda narrated that he went with Abū Maʿshar to visit al-Shaʿbī. His family said he was not home. Qatāda asked, "Where did he go?" His family answered, "We do not know." Qatāda disapprovingly said, "Are you saying he does not tell you where he goes?" They said, "Yes." Telling your family where you are decreases their worries if you are late and will keep both of you at ease, as they will be able to reach you if they need to.

6.8 Respect the Poor

If you come across a poor person at a gathering, or a poor person visited you at home or at work, do not look down upon him or her. Poverty is not a defect or a fault to be ashamed of, while lack of kindness and generosity is. Treat poor acquaintances or guests with honour and respect. Talk pleasantly to them, using the best of language. Again, poverty is not a vice, many who are poor are more honourable than the wealthy, and many who are penniless are preferred to the rich.

6.9 Exchanging Gifts

If a friend, a relative, or an acquaintance gives you a gift, thank them as soon as possible regardless of the value of the gift. It is good manner to show warm appreciation for such kind gesture and if you can, reciprocate with an appropriate gift. The Prophet ﷺ said, "Whoever does you a favour then reward him, if you can not reward him, pray for him."[67] The hadith calls upon the receivers to reciprocate within their means. The reward means a gift equivalent to that received; if that is not possible, then a simple gift will do; and if that is not at hand, then a sincere prayer would suffice.

It is recommended that the reward be better than the original gift. It is the essence of Islamic manners to return a nice gesture with a better one. A man brought Imām Abū Ḥanīfa a gift worth ten dirhams and the Imām presented him with a gift worth five hundred dirhams. The man was surprised and said, "But Imām, my gift was little, about a tenth of your gift." "Your gift is more valuable," the Imām answered. "You remembered me while I forgot you, I remembered you only after you had given me your gift. So your gift is better."

It is a bad manner to receive a gift and remain silent without a word of thanks, as if it is your due right to be presented with gifts. It is equally ill-mannered to delay that to a later time or until you are reminded of the gift.

Chapter Seven

COMMUNICATING WITH NON-MUSLIMS

7.1 Good Relations with Non-Muslims

As a Muslim, one should demonstrate to all people the goodness of Islam with gentle manners and kind behaviour. Bukhārī and Muslim reported the hadith of Anas, "None of you [perfectly] believes until he loves for his brother what he loves for himself." The version reported by Muslim says, "Unless he loves for his brother or neighbour, as he loves for himself."[68] The scholars commented that the word "brother" is used in the most common context, and thus means "brother" in humanity, including both Muslims and non-Muslims. A Muslim should love for his non-Muslim brother, as he loves for himself, to become a Muslim so as to enjoy the benefits of Islam and the rewards of Allah. A Muslim does an act of goodness when he prays for the guidance of his non-Muslim brothers just as he prays for his Muslim brothers to remain Muslims and to continue their devotion and adherence to Islam.

In Sūrat al-Mumtaḥina Allah said, *Allah forbid you not, with regard to those who do not fight you for your faith nor drive you out of your homes, to deal kindly and justly with them: For Allah loves those who are just. Allah only forbids you, with regard to those who fought you for your faith and drove you out of your homes and support others in driving you out, for turning to them for friendship and alliance. Those of you who do that are doing wrong* (Quran, 60:8).

Nothing prevents us from being kind, generous and helpful to non-Muslims as long as they do not demonstrate verbal or tangible animosity towards Islam. Hopefully, this will remove barriers between them and Islam and Muslims. If your neighbours happen to be non-Muslims, you must not forget good Islamic manners in dealing with neighbours - Muslims and non-Muslims alike. We may invite them to our homes, or accept their invitations, as long as this is done without breaking the rules of Islam.

7.2 The Opinion of Imām al-Qurṭubī

This positive attitude is not a license to abandon our distinct personality. It means we must be fair, kind and reasonable within ourselves and with our neighbours in all matters. In interpreting this, the great scholar of *tafsīr*, Imām al-Qurṭubī said, "This constitutes a consent by Allah to maintain amicable relationship with those who do not antagonize Muslims or attack them."

Imām al-Qurṭubī cited the opinion of ʿAbd al-Raḥmān ibn Zayd who said that this rule was in the beginning of Islam when fighting was not required, but later it was abrogated. Imām al-Qurṭubī also cited Qatāda who said this verse had been abrogated by the verse in Sūrat al-Tawba, *But when the sacred months are past, then fight the pagans wherever you find them* (Quran, 9:5).

After citing these two opinions and other similar ones, Imām al-Qurṭubī concluded by saying, "The majority of commentators have agreed that this verse has not been abrogated. They cited the story reported by Bukhārī and Muslim of Asmā' bint Abū Bakr when she asked the Prophet ﷺ if she could receive and be kind to her non-Muslim mother who visited her in Madinah and the Prophet ﷺ said, "Yes." It was said that this verse (Quran, 60:8) was revealed in this specific incident. Al-Mawardī and Abū Dāwūd reported that ʿĀmir ibn ʿAbdullāh ibn al-Zubayr narrated that his father told him that before accepting Islam Abū Bakr divorced his wife Qatīla, the mother of Asmā'. When the truce was held between the Prophet ﷺ and the pagans of Quraysh, the mother visited her daughter in Madinah and brought her a pair of earrings and other gifts. Asmā' was reluctant to accept the gifts before asking the Prophet ﷺ. In answer to her question, Allah revealed this verse.

When Allah says to deal kindly and justly with them, al-Farra said that Allah meant those who do not fight you, alluding to Khuzāʿa tribe who made a peace treaty with the Muslims not to fight them or assist those who fight them. Allah ordered Muslims to be kind and fair to them as per the terms of the agreement.

Qaḍī Abū Bakr ibn al-ʿArabī said that the expression of *qisṭ* [mentioned in the above verse] is not derived from *justice* but from *share*. This means you may give them a portion of your money to maintain cordial relationship. Justice is a duty toward all whether friends or foes.

7.3 Visiting Ill Non-Muslims

You may visit non-Muslims who fall ill, be they neighbours, relatives, co-workers, or business acquaintances. Imām Bukhārī reported that the Prophet ﷺ visited his non-Muslim uncle Abū Ṭālib on his death bed and urged him to embrace Islam.

Imām Bukhārī and Imām Aḥmad reported that Anas ibn Mālik said that a Jewish boy used to serve the Prophet ﷺ preparing his ablution and bringing him his shoes. The boy became ill, and the Prophet ﷺ went to visit him. He found him gravely ill with his father sitting by his side. The Prophet ﷺ invited the boy to Islam by asking him to say, "There is no God but Allah." The boy looked at his father who kept silent. The Prophet ﷺ repeated his request and the boy again looked at his father who told him, "Obey Abū'l-Qāsim." The boy just before dying said, "I bear witness that there is no God but Allah and that you are His Messenger." The Prophet ﷺ said, "I thank Allah for enabling me to save him." [69]

Commenting on the hadith, Ibn Ḥajar said this indicates many rules: Muslims are to be cordial with non-Muslims and are allowed to employ them and to visit them while sick. It allows the employment of youth, to offer them Islam if they are mature to make a decision, and to accept their conversion if they embrace Islam.

Similarly, Imām al-Badr al-ᶜAynī said this hadith provides us with the permission to visit ill non-Muslims especially if they are neighbours. Such a visit demonstrates the kindness of Islam and may encourage them to embrace it. The hadith also allows the employment of non-Muslims and encourages cordiality to them. It also consents to employing the youth, and implies the acceptance of their conversion to Islam. One may ask why the Prophet ﷺ offered Islam to this young boy under these conditions and in the presence of his father? The answer is this was his duty as ordered by Allah—to guide humanity to Islam.

7.4 Expressing Condolence to Non-Muslims

One may console grieving non-Muslims using appropriate expressions. Al-Qāḍī Abū Yūsuf said, at the end of his book *al-Kharaj,* that he asked Abū Ḥanīfa about how to console a Jew or a Christian who lost a child or a relative. Abū Ḥanīfa taught him to say, "Allah decreed death for all His creations. We ask Allah to make death the best fate to wait for. We all belong to Allah and to Him we all shall return. Be patient and endure this calamity."

Abū Yūsuf narrates that a Christian who used to attend the lectures of Ḥasan al-Baṣrī had died. Upon hearing this, Ḥasan went to console his brother. He said, "May Allah reward you for this calamity as He rewards your fellows. May Allah bless our death and make it the best fate to wait for. Be patient against the misfortunes." Therefore, one may say these kind words, reminding them of death as the inescapable fate with which we can do nothing about but accept and be patient.

In his book *Radd al-Mukhtār,* Imām Ibn ᶜĀbidīn quoted Shāfiᶜī scholars saying, "You may console Muslims on the death of a non-Muslim relative. On such occasion you may say, 'May Allah increase your rewards and patience.' You may console non-Muslims on the loss of a Muslim relative. On such occasions you may say, 'May Allah forgive your deceased and give you best condolence.' Consoling them on the loss of a non-Muslim you may say, 'May Allah compensate your loss.'" [70]

Chapter Eight

THE MANNERS OF EATING

8.1 The Importance of the Manners of Eating

The manners of eating are very important to learn and perfect since they are repeated many times a day. One must learn how to eat properly whether eating alone, with family or with friends. To avoid pretences, you with your family should practice proper eating manners until it becomes a natural part of your behaviour.

8.2 The Manners of Eating

There are certain indispensable table manners, they are as follows: Say *Bismillāh* ["In the name of Allah"] when you start and thank Allah by saying *al-Ḥamdulillāh* [Praise be to Allah] when you finish. Eat what is in front of you. Eat using your right hand. ʿAmr ibn Salama, a Companion of the Prophet ﷺ, tells this story, "I was a young boy, and my hand used to go all over the plate. The Prophet ﷺ saw me do this and said, 'My son, say *Bismillāh*, eat with your right, and eat what is in front of you.'"[71] On another occasion a hypocrite was eating with his left hand when the Prophet ﷺ saw him and advised him to eat with his right. "But I cannot," the man lied arrogantly. The Prophet ﷺ said, "May it be so," and the hypocrite was not able to lift his right hand again.[72]

The Companions of the Prophet ﷺ followed his example in stressing the use of the right hand while eating. During ʿUmar's Khilāfa, he saw a man eating with his left hand, and similarly advised him to eat with his right. The man answered, "My right is busy!" ʿUmar repeated his request, and the man repeated his answer. ʿUmar asked him, "Busy with what?" The man informed him that it had been severed in one of the battles. ʿUmar blamed himself for neglecting such disabled people and ordered the treasurer to provide the man with a servant to help him.

When eating with your hand, use three fingers with small morsels, lifting it gently with ease to your mouth. Keep your mouth closed while eating to avoid unnecessary noises. To eat on the floor is closer to what the Prophet ﷺ used to do. However, there is no problem to eat at a table. Imām al-Ghazālī said, "To eat at a table is to make eating easier and there is nothing against that." Do not start eating ahead of the elders or the nobles. If you are the elder, do not commence eating before everyone is at the table.

It is preferred that eating should not be conducted in silence. It is a good manner to talk during meals. The topics should be pleasant and suitable to be discussed whilst eating. At the end of the meal, when the hands are to be washed, the elders or the nobles should be asked to proceed first. At the end of a meal, thank Allah as narrated in the hadith reported by Abū Dāwūd and al-Nasā'ī in *Aʿmāl al-Yawm wa al-Layla,* "Praise be to Allah who fed us and provided us with drink and guided us to Islam."[73] It is very appropriate to make a prayer for your hosts. Imām Muslim reported that Al-Miqdād ibn al-Aswad narrated that the Prophet ﷺ said, "May Allah feed those who have fed us, and provide drinks to those who provided us with it."[74]

Do not express your disapproval or dislike of the food placed in front of you; either eat it or pass it over quietly. Abū Hurayra reported, "The Prophet ﷺ never expressed his dislike of a food. If he liked it, he ate it, and if he disliked it, he set it aside."[75]

Do not put in your plate more than you can eat, for your leftovers could be thrown away and wasted, and this is against Islamic teachings. Put smaller portions twice rather than one large portion that you will not eat. The Prophet ﷺ did not approve of leaving any food on a plate. He said, "You don't know which portion is blessed."[76] Food is a blessing of Allah; to misuse it is contrary to Islam. Do not forget the poor and the needy who need the portion you are throwing away.

8.3 The Manners of Drinking

Drinking manners are no less important. To start in the name of Allah is a must. Likewise, use your right hand to drink. Abū Dāwūd and Tirmidhī related that Ḥafṣa said, "The Prophet ﷺ used his right hand for eating and drinking. He used his left for other things [such as personal hygiene]."[77] Do not pour your drink down your throat in one gulp; drink it in three sips. Ibn ᶜAbbās reported that the Prophet ﷺ said, "Do not drink like a camel. Drink twice or thrice. Say the name of Allah before drinking, and thank Allah after finishing."[78] Do not blow or breath into your glass; this will irritate others. Ibn ᶜAbbās reported that the Prophet ﷺ forbade exhaling in a glass or puffing into it.[79]

Do not drink directly from the jug or the container; besides being un-hygienic, you could irritate others who want to drink after you. Abū Hurayra narrated that the Prophet ﷺ forbade drinking directly from the mouth of the sheepskin or the flask.[80]

8.4 Avoid Overeating

Modesty is the crown of sensible people. Keep this crown on your head if invited to a feast or if you are presented with food or drink. Do not be greedy consuming food as if you have not eaten for a long time, or as if you have not seen such excellent food before. Do not sample every dish on the table. People, including generous hosts, disapprove of greedy eaters. Therefore, be reasonable and moderate in enjoying the generosity of your hosts.

8.5 Gold and Silver Cutlery

Do not eat using golden or silver plates or cutlery. This goes against the spirit of Islamic modesty; pomposity is not an Islamic trait. Bukhārī narrated that Ḥudhayfa said the Prophet ﷺ said, "Do not drink in golden or silver cups nor eat in such plates."[81] If you are a guest, simply ask your host to replace it with another one.

Chapter Nine

WEDDING MANNERS

9.1 Weddings Parties

Weddings Parties are part of the Prophet's ﷺ tradition. If invited to a marriage ceremony or a wedding celebration, you should accept the invitation unless you are aware it may include prohibited acts. Attending a wedding is part of the *sunna*, as Islam considers marriage an act of worship and obedience to Allah. Islam endorses performing marriage ceremonies in the mosque. Muslim jurists based this on a collection of *aḥadīth*. The first is reported by Tirmidhī and Ibn Māja, "Announce the marriage, execute it at the mosques and celebrate it with drums."[82] In another hadith, reported by Imām Aḥmad and al-Ḥākim, the Prophet ﷺ said, "Announce marriage." In a third hadith, reported by Aḥmad, Tirmidhī, al-Nasā'ī and Ibn Māja, the Prophet ﷺ said, "The difference between a *ḥalāl* [lawful] and a *ḥaram* [forbidden] relationship is [its announcement with] celebrations and drums."[83]

There is no dispute among Muslim scholars that in a wedding celebration, the Prophet ﷺ allowed women to use drums. The most valid opinion among many scholars is that men can also use drums in order to publicize the marriage thus making it known near and far. The noble Islamic purpose of such publicity is to distinguish between an evil and illicit relationship and a noble and desirable marriage.

Attending a wedding is one of the duties of brotherhood among Muslims. It fulfils the requirement of announcing and witnessing a marriage, and gives us the opportunity to join our brothers or sisters as they complete the second half of Islam, praying they will remain observant of the first half. Attending a wedding also honours the husband and wife by having their relatives and friends share in their joy and happiness. It blesses them when guests pray to Allah for their righteousness, success, affluence and prosperity.

9.2 The Manners of Attending Weddings

If invited, attend the celebration with the intention of participating in a blessed occasion and a delightful celebration, as the Prophet ﷺ taught. Dress appropriately for this joyous occasion. The Prophet's ﷺ Companions used to dress nicely when visiting each other. If you initiate or share in a talk, make sure it fits the happy occasion and does not include depressing and distasteful subjects that spoil the occasion. Muslims should always be wise and considerate.

It is recommended that you congratulate the bride and bridegroom, by repeating what the Prophet ﷺ said, "May Allah bless you and bless your spouse and may Allah unite you with prosperity."[84] Do not use the commonly used phrase "With comfort and children," because this was the phrase used by the people of *jāhiliyya*. The Prophet ﷺ prohibited such a saying, and Allah, with His blessing, replaced it by the prayer of His Prophet ﷺ. Bukhārī reported that ᶜĀ'isha said, "When the Prophet ﷺ married me, my mother led me into the house where women of Anṣār were celebrating. They congratulated me and wished me prosperity, blessing and 'best of fortune.'"

Islam permits women to celebrate weddings by singing joyous songs, accompanied by a drumbeat. Such poems and songs should not promote lust, lewd desire or portray physical beauty. Instead, they should sing delightful and decent songs to express their happiness with the marriage. ᶜĀ'isha said, "A bride was led to her Anṣārī husband. The Prophet ﷺ then said, "O ᶜĀ'isha, did you not have merriment? The Anṣār love fun."[85] He was referring to the singing and beating of drums.

Ibn Ḥajar reported in his book *Fatḥ al-Bārī* that ʿĀ'isha recalled that the Prophet ﷺ asked, "Why did you not send with her [the bride] a singer girl to sing with a drum beat?" I said, "Singing what?" He answered: Songs sung at weddings must be decent and contain similar wholesome and seemly meanings. Songs of lust, passion and immorality should be avoided.

Chapter Ten

VISITING THE SICK

10.1 Visiting a Sick Person

The mercy that Allah created in human beings prompts us to sympathize with those who fall ill. Bukhārī narrated a hadith by Abū Hurayra that the Prophet ﷺ emphasized that human mercy is a minute continuation of the mercy of Allah. The Prophet ﷺ said, "Allah divided mercy into a hundred portions. He kept ninety-nine portions with Him, and released one portion on earth. It is from this portion that creatures have mercy [on each other], such that a mare would lift her hoof lest it hit her child."[86]

It is the duty of every Muslim to visit his or her fellow Muslim in time of illness; this will enhance and nourish the bond of Islam and the brotherhood among them. As a committed Muslim, one should not undervalue the great reward from Allah. Imām Muslim reported that the Messenger of Allah ﷺ said, "A Muslim visiting a sick brother will continue to be in the *khurfa* of Paradise until he comes back home. He was asked, "What is the *khurfa* of Paradise?" He answered, "This means the harvest of Paradise."[87]

Likewise, Imām Aḥmad and Ibn Ḥibbān (in his book of authentic *aḥadīth*) reported that the Messenger ﷺ said, "A visitor walking to visit a patient will be walking into the mercy of Allah. When the visitor sits with the patient, both will be engulfed in Allah's mercy until the visitor's return."

Muslims in Andalusia were very articulate in their charitable endeavours and endowments. In taking care of the sick, they set up charitable funds to pay two people of each neighbourhood who were admired for their piety to visit the homes of the sick to try to raise their morale by praying for them and giving them hope of recovery.

10.2 Praying for the Sick

It is very appropriate to say prayers for the sick, asking Allah to bless them with recovery and help them through their sickness. Bukhārī and Muslim reported that ᶜĀ'isha said, "If someone fell sick the Prophet ﷺ would pass his right hand over them while saying the following prayer, 'O Allah, Lord of mankind, take away the suffering, bring the recovery, no cure but your cure leaves no illness.'"[88] In another hadith, reported by Bukhārī, Ibn ᶜAbbās said that the Prophet ﷺ when visiting a sick person would say, "Be patient, may Allah cleanse you."

Do not discount the importance of the prayers of the pious. Allah has endowed some of His servants with blessings that could bring recovery and raise morale. However, abandoning treatment in favour of prayers is contrary to the Prophet's ﷺ teachings: "Servants of Allah, seek cure, for He who created sickness created the cure." In another hadith, the Prophet ﷺ prescribed reciting the Quran and giving charity as part of the cure. He said, "Treat your ill with Quran, prayers and alms." Allah in the Quran says, *We have sent down of this Quran that which is a cure and mercy for believers* (Quran, 17:82).

Prayers from a pious, clear heart are very effective. In 1388 AH /1968, while visiting Madinah, my eldest daughter, who was thirteen years old at the time, was diagnosed with appendicitis. The doctors left no doubt that she should be operated on right away. That meant our Ḥajj would be disrupted. I went to a pious, humble and not well-known shaykh and asked him to pray for her and for us. To our relief and to the amazement of the doctors she became well and fit to travel within two days.

10.3 The Length of the Visit

Following certain etiquette will make your visit to sick persons refreshing and reflective. Your duty is to ease their pain and make them more aware of the rewards they will gain in return for their suffering and endurance. Make your visit brief, as sick persons may not withstand long visits or actually dislike them. The length of the visit should not be longer than the time between the two sermons of Friday. In this respect, it was said that the visit should be long enough to convey your salām and wishes, to ask the sick how he or she is doing, to pray for their recovery and to leave immediately after bidding them farewell:

> If you visit a patient say your greeting
> And immediately you should say, 'Good-bye'
> The best visit is every third day
> And should not be longer than a blink of an eye
> Do not bother the patient with many questions
> Two or three words will get you all along.[89]

At the end of his book of Mālikī *Fiqh al-Kāfī*, Imām Ibn ʿAbd al-Barr said, "Whether you visit a healthy or an ill person, you should sit where you are told, for hosts know better how to ensure the privacy of their home. Visiting an ill person is a confirmed *sunna*. The best visit is the shortest. Visitors should not sit too long with the ill person, unless they are close friends and the ill person enjoys their company."

10.4 The Manners of Visiting a Sick Person

The visitor should wear clean clothes with a fresh scent in order to make the patient feel better both spiritually and physically. At the same time, it is improper to wear fancy clothes that are more appropriate for parties and festivities. Likewise, wearing a strong perfume may annoy the sick.

Visitors should keep their conversation light and avoid gloomy subjects that might exacerbate the patient's distress. Avoid conveying bad news, such as a failing business, a death or similar stressful events. Also, visitors should not inquire about the details of illness unless the visitor is a specialized physician. Similarly, visitors should not recommend to a patient any food or medicine that might have helped them or someone else. Such recommendation, or rather interference, may lead the ill person out of ignorance or desperation to try it, causing further complication or even death.

Do not criticize or object to the treatment prescribed by the physicians in the presence of the ill person, for it will shake his trust in his doctors. If you are a specialized physician, you may want to discuss the case and its treatment privately with the doctor in charge.

10.5 How the Ill Express Their Complaints

It is recommended that when asked how is he feeling, a sick person should start by thanking Allah and then proceed to list his complaints. This is to avoid the appearance of complaining against Allah's will. This was the etiquette of the *Tābiᶜīn* as reported by al-Khaṭīb al-Baghdādī in his *Tārīkh Baghdād*. In the biography of ᶜAbd al-Raḥmān al-Ṭabīb, who was the physician of both Imām Aḥmad and Bishr al-Ḥāfī, the physician recounted that both Imām Aḥmad and Bishr became sick and he treated them at the same place, probably a hospital. "When I visited Bishr, I asked how he felt, and he would start by thanking Allah before saying I have this pain or that complaint. When I visited Imām Aḥmad and asked how he felt, he would say, 'I feel all right.' One day I told him, 'Your brother Bishr is also ill, but when I ask him of his condition, he thanks Allah first, then tells me his condition.' Imām Aḥmad said, 'Please ask him where he got this from.' I answered, 'His respectability makes me reluctant to ask.' Imām Aḥmad said, 'Tell him your brother, Abū ᶜAbdullāh, asks where did you get this.' ᶜAbd al-Raḥmān asked Bishr as told. Bishr replied, 'Abū ᶜAbdullāh wants everything with authority. I heard this from Azhar who heard it from Ibn ᶜAwn who heard it from

Ibn Sīrīn; if a person thanked Allah before complaining, it will not be a complaint but as if it is telling the acts of Allah.'" ʿAbd al-Raḥmān said, "I told this to Imām Aḥmad. After that, if asked how he felt, he would start by thanking Allah, and then describing his complaints."[90]

The answer of Bishr indicates that when asked about their health, the sick preferably should praise Allah first then explain their condition. Therefore, it is not considered complaining against the acts of Allah.

10.6 Reflections on Illness

If you become ill, remember that without illness we would not recognize the blessing of good health. Even sickness could bring blessings that only later we will become aware of. It could bring forced period of reflection and review of your lifestyle and the way you conduct your affairs. Many go through difficulty and times of trials to discover later that indeed that was a blessing in disguise.

Chapter Eleven

MANNERS FOR TRAVELING

Travel has become an essential part of the life of many people on this earth. Islam teaches us some particular manners, spiritual and practical, that Muslims are advised to follow to ensure, with the help of Allah, a safe and pleasant journey. They are as follows:

1. Study and review the rules of prayers and fasting for the traveler, including the rules of *masḥ,* combining prayers, direction to Makkah [Qibla], etc.

2. It is advisable, if possible, not to travel alone. The Prophet ﷺ advised strongly against it when he said in the hadith narrates by Ibn ᶜUmar and reported by Bukhari "Had people known what I know about travelling alone, no traveller would journey at night. In another hadith reported by Abū Dāwūd, Tirmidhī, and Nasā'ī, he said, "A lone traveller is [prone] to the devil, two travellers are [prone to] to two devils and three are indeed travellers."

3. Before starting your journey, clip your fingers nails, have a hair cut and trim your beard. Even when travelling a Muslim must appear in best of shape. In the hadith narrated by Sahl ibn al-Hanzalia and reported by Muslim the Prophet ﷺ advised a group of young companions to be in the best of shape like a beauty mark among people.

4. Before leaving your house, on your journey, you should pray two *rakᶜas*. Al-Muṭᶜim bin Al-Miqdām Al-Sanᶜanī, a follower (*Tābiᶜī*) who mostly narrated the hadiths of the followers (*Tābiᶜīn*), said that the Prophet said: "When travelling there is

nothing better to leave behind at home than two *rak*ᶜ*as* prayed there at the on-set."[91] This hadith could be construed to mean the prayers of guidance (*Istikhāra*).

5. If you stop during your travel, it might be advisable to pray two *rak*ᶜ*as* before continuing the rest of the journey. Anas ibn Malik said: "When the Prophet stopped at a place during a journey, he would not leave that place before bidding it farewell with two *rak*ᶜ*as*.[92]

6. Some scholars recommended reciting, in the two *rak*ᶜ*as*, Sūra Al-Kāfirūn (Chapter 99) and Al-Ikhlāṣ (Chapter 112), as they are statements of disassociation from disbelief and a declaration of the Oneness of Allah. Other scholars recommended reciting Sūras Al-Falaq and Al-Nās (Chapters 113 and 114) as they include circumspection and seeking refuge from Allah (saw).

7. After concluding the two *rak*ᶜ*as* at home, you may recite Ayah Al-Kursī (verse 2:255) before leaving the house. It is has been narrated that whoever reads Ayah Al-Kursī before exiting his house no harm will befall him till his return. Abū Hurayra narrated that the Prophet said: "Whoever reads, in the morning, Ayah Al-Kursī and the first three verses of Sūra Al-Mu'minīn (Chapter 40), he will not be harmed by anything he detests until the evening. And whoever reads it in the evening; he will not be harmed by anything he detests till the morning."[93]

8. It is recommended that, after reciting the verses, to pray to Allah with a sincere, tender, and present heart. Ask Allah for protection for yourself and your family. One of the best prayers to say in this regard after praising Allah and praying for the Prophet: "Oh Allah, Your help I seek, I entrust myself to You. Oh Allah ease obstacles for me, ease the difficulties of my travel, grant me the good more than I ask for, and send the bad away from me."

"My Lord! Cleanse my heart, and make my issue easy on me. O Allah, I seek your protection and entrust you with myself, my faith, my family, and my relatives and all what you gave me and whether for the hereafter or this life. O Allah protect us all from every harm; you are the generous. Praise be to Allah the lord of the universe and may He reward our Prophet Muhammad, his kin and followers.

9. When standing up after the two *rakᶜas* and the afore said prayer, you may say what Anas has narrated that the Prophet before commencing a journey would complete his prayer and would say when getting up from his prayer: " O Allah, I pursue You, and I seek shelter in You. O Allah shield me from what worries me and from what I am not aware of. O Allah! Increase my piety, forgive my bad deeds, and guide me to the good wherever I go"[94]

10. When leaving the house, bid your family and dear ones farewell and entrust them to Allah as Abū Hurayra narrated that the prophet said: "Whoever wants to travel, he should tell those he is leaving behind 'I entrust you to Allah, whose trusts are never lost." Imam Ahmad stated in the Musnad and Al Nasā'ī and Ibn Ḥibbān, reported that ᶜAbdullah ibn ᶜUmar narrated, that the Prophet said: "When Allah is entrusted with something. He looks after it."[95]

11. Family or friends who are seeing-off the traveler should say what Anas narrated that when a man came to the Prophet and asked him: "Prophet of Allah! I am preparing to travel, so provide me with your prayers." The Prophet replied, "May Allah provide you with piety." The man said, "Please give me more" The prophet answered, "And may Allah forgive your sins" the man once again said, "Provide me more" the prophet replied, "and may He bring the good wherever you are."[96] Imam Ibn Dawūd in the Sunan reported that Abdullah Ibn ᶜUmar said to Kaz'a "Let me tell you the Prophet's farewell to me: 'I entrust Allah with your faith, your trust, and your deeds."[97] The trust here means family and assets and all valuables left behind.

12. If you saw traveller off should ask him to pray for you.

Abū Dāwūd and Tirmidhi reported a hadith narrated by ʿUmar ibn Al-Khaṭṭāb "I asked the Prophet to permit me to perform Umra and he permitted me to do so and said to me 'Brother, don't forget us in your prayers' a word that is to me worth more than the whole earth." The prayers of the pious traveler will be accepted by Allah, as has been narrated by Abū Hurayra: "Prayers that will be answered beyond doubt; that of the wronged and of the traveler."[98]

13. When you ride a car, a plane, a ship, or an animal, you should say the prayers of the Prophet that ʿAbdullah ibn ʿUmar narrated. When he rode his camel, he would repeat Takbir thrice and then he would say: "Praise be to the One who put this under our disposal, and we shall not associate with Him, and to our Lord is our return. Oh Allah! In our travel we ask You for piety and the deeds you like. Oh Allah! Make this journey easy and shorten its distance. Oh Allah! You are the companion of our travel, and the guardian of our family, wealth, and children. Oh Allah! We ask you to shield us from the hardship of travel, the unkempt appearance and a bad end befalling our wealth and children."

14. Upon his return, the Prophet ﷺ would repeat these prayers adding to it: "We return, repentant, God-worshiping; and to our lord thankful."[99]

15. If you pass-by a town then, whether you want to stop or pass through it, you say the prayers Suhayb narrated. That upon seeing a city he intended to enter the Prophet ﷺ would say: "O Allah, Lord of the seven heavens and all it covers, Lord of the seven earths and what they hold, Lord of the devils and what they misguide, and Lord of the winds and what they blow. I ask You the good of this town, the good of its people, and the good of what it holds. And I seek refuge from its evil, the evil of its people and the evil it holds."[100]

16. It is the tradition of the Prophet ﷺ to return to your home as soon as you finished your travel. Abū Hurayra narrated

that the Prophet ﷺ said "Travel is akin to punishment as it prevents you from having your [regular] food and drink. If you performed your task then hasten back to your family"[101]

17. Utilize travel time: When packing for a trip don't forget to take with you a copy of the Quran and useful reading material, preferably on two diverse subject in case you get bored. Travel time, away from distractions, is very good to read with concentration.

18. Keep a light-weight prayer mat handy in your hand luggage, should you need to pray on the road. Take with you a compass or a similar tool to know the direction of Mecca (Qibla)

19. When you reach your destination, unpack right away to keep your cloths neat and your belongings tidy. This will help you maintain good appearance that will impress those whom you meet. It is also the tradition of the Prophet ﷺ who as Anas, his servant, said: once he arrived at a place he would not even commence prayers until they bring down loads off their animals.[12]

20. Bring a gift to your dear ones and friends. The Prophet ﷺ said "Exchange gifts; exchange love." This a good general practice that has been practiced more by travellers.

Chapter Twelve

CONDOLENCES

12.1 Breaking Unpleasant News

If you must give the undesirable news of a tragic accident, or the death of a close relative or a dear friend, break the news in a way that decreases its impact and makes it as mild and gentle as possible. For example, in the case of a death, you may say, "Recently, I learned that Mrs. Aḥmad has been very sick. Unfortunately her condition has worsened lately. Today, I learned she has passed away. May the mercy of Allah be with her."

One should start by giving the name of the person in question. Do not break the news of a death by asking, "Do you know who died today?" This unduly manner frightens the listeners and prompts them to expect the worst, like the death of someone who is very close to them. Instead, mention the name of the dead person before breaking the tragic news of the death, this will make the news more bearable by softening its impact and reducing the listener's apprehension.

Likewise, convey the news of any tragedy (such as a fire, drowning, car accident, etc.) in a similar fashion. Prepare the listener for the news in a way that minimizes its impact. Mention the name of the affected person in a kind way, not a shocking way. Some people have weak hearts and such bad news may cause them to faint and collapse.

Choose the appropriate time to convey such news. It should not take place at a meal, before going to sleep or during an illness.

Compassion and tactfulness are the best qualities you will need to handle such a situation.

12.2 Expressing Condolence is a Courtesy and a Duty

Parting among loved ones is the rule of Allah in His creations, al-Ḥāfiẓ al-Mundhirī reported the hadith, "Love whoever you will, for you will part." Along these same lines, poets have said:

> We are but guests with our families
> Staying a while and leaving them
>
> Wealth and parents are but trusts
> Inevitably, one day trusts will be recalled
>
> The children of this life will all part
> Until they meet together again in the Hereafter

One wise poet listed eight stages we all pass through, and no one is spared:

> Happiness and sorrow; meeting and separation
> Suffering and ease; illness and well being

Another poet said:

> Make endurance my friend,
> and leave painful sorrow
> You are not alone.
> Everyone lost, or will lose, a loved one

If a relative or a close friend of one of your relatives or friends dies, hasten to offer your condolences. You have the moral obligation toward your relatives and friends of alleviating their suffering. If you can, you should attend the funeral and the burial at the cemetery. Aside from being a highly rewarded gesture of sympathy, it could be an effective and stern admonition, a lesson reminding you of the inevitability of death:

> Your life taught me many lessons
> Today, your death taught me the most important lesson

Bukhārī reported that the Prophet ﷺ said, "The rights of a Muslim towards his brethren are five: to return a greeting, to visit them when ill, to attend their funerals, to answer their invitations, and to bless them after they sneeze."[103] Imām Aḥmad reported that the Prophet ﷺ said, "Visit the sick and follow the procession of funerals; you will remember the Hereafter."

Condolences alleviate the sense of grieving that befalls the family of the deceased. This is achieved by encouraging them to remain composed and to trust in Allah's great reward. Allah says in Sūrat al-Baqara, *And give glad tidings to those who patiently endure, who say, when afflicted with a disaster, "Truly to Allah we belong and to Him is our return." They are those on whom descend blessings and mercy of their Lord, and they are the guided ones* (Quran, 2:155-57). Condolence includes praying for the help and pardon of the deceased, as they will receive the benefit of such prayers. Condolence is a sincere expression of ones sympathy and sorrow at these stressful moments. Ibn Māja and al-Bayhaqī reported, with a fair ranking, the hadith, "A Muslim who consoles other Muslims suffering from a calamity will be awarded a dress of dignity by Allah on the day of Judgment."[104]

12.3 Expressing Condolences and Sympathy

When offering condolences about a plight that befalls a relative, a friend or an acquaintance, it is very appropriate to pray for the dead. Say a prayer similar to that reported by Muslim to have been articulated by the Messenger ﷺ to Umm Salama at the death of her husband, "O Allah, forgive Abū Salama, elevate his status among the guided people, and look after the family that he left behind. O our Lord of the universe, forgive us and him, comfort him in his grave, and lighten his stay."[105] Your conversation with the anguished persons should be aimed at mitigating their agony by mentioning the reward of patience, the transitory nature of life on earth, and that the Hereafter is everlasting life.

In this respect, it is desirable to quote certain verses of the Quran, the sayings of the Prophet ﷺ or some of the well-spoken condolences of our ancestors. You may mention the words of Allah, *And give glad tidings to those who patiently endure, who say, when afflicted with a disaster, "Truly to Allah we belong and to Him is our return." They are those on whom descend blessings and mercy of their Lord, and they are the guided ones* (Quran, 2:155-57). Or you may quote another verse from the Quran, *Every soul shall have a taste of death and only on the Day of Judgment shall you be paid your full recompense. Only those who are saved far from the fire and admitted to the Garden will have attained the object [of life], for the life of this world is but goods and chattels of deception* (Quran, 3:185). Similarly Allah said, *All that is on earth will perish. But abiding forever is the Face of your Lord, Most Gracious and Most Generous* (Quran, 55:26-27).

You may mention some of sayings of the Prophet ﷺ reported by Muslim and others, "O Allah, reward my calamity and replace my loss with a better one."[106] Likewise, the saying of the Prophet ﷺ reported by Bukhārī and Muslim, "To Allah belongs what He gives, and to Him belongs what He takes; it is He that gives, and for every matter He prescribed a certain destiny."[107] Bukhārī and Muslim reported that when the Prophet ﷺ mourned the death of his son Ibrāhīm, he said, "My eyes are tearful, my heart is full of anguish, but we will only say what pleases our Lord. O Ibrāhīm, your loss filled us with sorrow."[108]

If you are being condoled you may want to reciprocate these prayers. Imām Aḥmad ibn Ḥanbal used to say, "May Allah answer your prayers and shower His mercy on both of us."

Also, it is very appropriate in this regard to use some of the traditional sayings of our Muslim forefathers. ʿUmar ibn al-Khaṭṭāb used to say, "Everyday we are told that this person or that has just died. One day it will be said, 'ʿUmar has died.'" You may also allude to the saying of the just Khalīfa ʿUmar ibn ʿAbd al-ʿAzīz, "A person who is not separated from Adam by a living father is indeed fast approaching death." The honoured *Tābiʿī* Ḥasan al-Baṣrī said, "O son of Adam, you are nothing but a mere collection of days. Whenever a day passes by, a part of you passes away." He also said, "Allah ordained that the ultimate resting place of believers will be paradise no less." He reflected that, saying, "Death made life tasteless for the wise. Sadness in life regenerates many rewards." His student Mālik ibn Dinār said, "The wedding of those who fear Allah is the Day of Judgment." A poet said:

Content we are passing the days
But every day is taking us away

Another poet said:

In offering condolences, we trust not to live long
But the manners of this religion we follow along
The consoled and the consoling may live today
Tomorrow though, both will vanish away

A suitable poem in this regard:

We die and live every night and day
One day we will die and move away

Another poem describes how oblivious humans can be to death:

Life is but a ship afloat
We think it's still, but running is the boat

I have quoted all these appropriate mourning quotations because I have witnessed many inappropriate conversations by people offering sympathy. Mourning hearts are depressed with anguish and sorrow. Be sensitive and select a suitable topic for your conversation. Attempt to lift the spirits of the bereaved family. The great scholar Manṣūr ibn Zazān said, "Sorrow and sadness will increase rewards." Ḥasan al-Baṣrī pointed out that this painful state will gradually pass away, but our sins will remain with us forever. He said, "Every sadness will diminish, except sadness over sins." The great scholar, ʿAṭā' ibn Abī Muslim pointed out that life is full of challenges and events, "A believer will not be happy for one complete day."

12.4 Sending flowers and reading Quran during funerals

At the death of a dear person, many people bring flowers and wreaths, and after proceeding with the funeral they take them to the home of the deceased. They buy the best flowers to show their deep sympathy and concern. To do this is forbidden, whether presenting it at the funeral, accompanying the funeral with it or bringing it to the house of the deceased. This wasteful imitation of some non-Muslims is an unwholesome innovation that should be avoided. Those who do such a thing will have no reward from Allah. To the contrary, they will be questioned for such meaningless waste.

Another misguided innovation is having the car carrying the deceased broadcast through speakers a recording of the Holy Quran, as if announcing the passing away of the deceased. Thoughtfulness, humbleness, remembrance, reflection, awareness of Allah and prayers for mercy should characterize the funeral procession. No sad music or religious chant should accompany funeral. These two rules should be followed and made known to make Muslims aware of the right way.

12.5 Reading the Quran During a Gathering of Condolence

It has become common among many Muslims for the family of the deceased to invite or hire a *ḥāfiẓ* [someone who has memorized the Quran] to recite the Quran during a gathering for condolence. A better alternative could be to bring the thirty parts of the Quran, and for each person to read at least one part, thus reading the whole Quran and forwarding the reward to the deceased. The Ḥanafī school of *fiqh* allows this practice based on its understanding of certain *aḥadīth*. Our forefathers did not collectively practice this tradition and people began this practice to avoid the trivial talk that became so characteristic of such gatherings. The Quran is full of wisdom and reminders; hence, reading the Quran became a better alternative.

Appendix

AUTHOR'S BIOGRAPHY

Shaykh ʿAbd al-Fattaḥ Abū Ghuddah was one of the most renowned Islamic scholars of our era. His renown spread all over the world from Brunei to North America for his outstanding achievements in the field of *daʿwa* and his scholarly works on Hadith, *Fiqh* and other Islamic studies.

Shaykh ʿAbd al-Fattaḥ ibn Muḥammad ibn Bashīr ibn Ḥasan Abū Ghuddah, may Allah bless him, was born in the city of Aleppo in the north of Syria on 17th of Rajab 1336 AH/1917 CE to a family whose lineage goes back to the great Companion Khālid ibn al-Walīd. The name Abū Ghuddah is relatively recent; other branches of the family hold the names of Sabbagh and Maqsud. Like many families in Aleppo, the business of the Shaykh's family for generations was the production of fabrics and trading in textiles. His father, Muḥammad, was well known for his piety and adherence to Islam. Bashir, his grandfather, was one of the biggest traders of textiles in Aleppo.

HIS SEARCH FOR KNOWLEDGE

The Shaykh's grandfather sensed his intelligence and took care of his education and enrolled him for four years at the Islamic Arab Institute in Aleppo. After working in the family business for a few years, he enrolled at the *Khesrevia Madrasa* (now known as *Sharʿiyyah* Secondary School) in 1356/1936 at the age of nineteen. He graduated in 1362/1942, and in 1364/1944 he left for

Egypt to continue his pursuit of knowledge at al-Azhar, Cairo. He obtained a BA in *Sharīʿa* in 1368/1948 and a diploma in psychology and methods of teaching, graduating from al-Azhar in 1370/1950.

HIS TEACHERS

In Syria, the following scholars were among the most prominent of his teachers:

• Shaykh Muḥammad Rāghib al-Tabbākh (1877-1951): A scholar of Hadith and History who published and wrote many books, most importantly were his seven volumes biographical history of Aleppo *Iʿlām al-Nubalā; bi Tārīkh Ḥalab al-Shahba.*

• Shaykh Aḥmad ibn Muḥammad al-Zarqa (1869-1937): A scholar of *Fiqh* and *Uṣūl al-Fiqh* and a prominent Ḥanafī jurist.

• Shaykh ʿĪsā al-Bayanūnī (1874-1942): A scholar of Shāfiʿī *Fiqh* and *Adab*. He was one of the Shaykh's earliest teachers, and his mosque was a minute's walk from the Shaykh's house. His piety and nearness to Allah left lasting impressions on the Shaykh. His son, Shaykh Aḥmad, was the closest friend to the Shaykh, and his grandsons were students of Shaykh ʿAbd al-Fattaḥ.

• Shaykh Muḥammad al-Ḥakīm (1904-1980): A scholar of Ḥanafī *Fiqh* and the Muftī of the Ḥanafīs in Aleppo.

• Shaykh Asʿad Ibājī (1895-1972): A scholar of Shāfiʿī *Fiqh* and the Muftī of the Shāfiʿīs in Aleppo.

• Shaykh Aḥmad ibn Muḥammad al-Kurdī (1885-1957): A recognized Muftī and scholar of Ḥanafī *Fiqh*.

• Shaykh Muḥammad Najīb Sirājuddīn (1876-1954): A scholar of *Tafsīr* and *Fiqh* and a prominent orator. He is the father of Shaykh ʿAbdullāh Sirājuddīn; a colleague of the Shaykh and a revered Shaykh in Aleppo.

• Shaykh Muṣṭafā al-Zarqa (1901-1999): The son of Shaykh Aḥmad al-Zarqa, and a great scholar in *Fiqh*, Comparative *Fiqh*, Arabic Grammar and Literature.

In Egypt, the following scholars were among the most prominent of his teachers:

- Shaykh Muḥammad al-Khiḍr Ḥusayn (1876-1958): A great scholar of *Tafsīr*, comparative and Mālikī *Fiqh*, Arabic Literature and the Grand Shaykh of al-Azhar.

- Shaykh ʿAbd al-Ḥalīm Maḥmūd (1907-1978): A great scholar of *Tafsīr*, *Uṣūl al Fiqh*, *Adab*, and Arabic literature and the Grand Shaykh of al-Azhar.

- Shaykh Maḥmūd ibn Muḥammad Shaltūt (1893-1963). A great scholar of *Tafsīr* and *Fiqh* who later became the Grand Shaykh of Al-Azhar.

He also met many other scholars, greatly benefiting and learning from them, most prominent among them were:

- Shaykh Muṣṭafā Ṣabrī (1869-1954): The last of *Shaykh al-Islām* of the Ottoman Khilāfa. He lived in poverty and dignity in exile in Egypt after the Kemalist revolution. A scholar of Hadith, *Uṣūl al-Fiqh,* Ḥanafī and Comparative *Fiqh*, Philosophy, and Politics.

- Shaykh Muḥammad Zāhid al-Kawtharī (1879-1952): An Ottoman scholar who was the Secretary of *Shaykh al-Islam* in Turkey. He lived in poverty and dignity in exile in Egypt after the Kemalist revolution. A scholar of Hadith, *Uṣūl al-Fiqh,* Ḥanafī and Comparative *Fiqh*. He wrote and published many Islamic books.

- Imām Shahīd Ḥasan a-Banna (1906-1949): The founder of the Muslim Brotherhood who revived the call to Allah and the understanding of Islam as a comprehensive way of life.

- Shaykh Aḥmad ibn ʿAbd al-Raḥmān al-Banna (1885-1958): The father of the founder of the Muslim Brotherhood and a scholar of Hadith and Ḥanafī *Fiqh*.

• Shaykh ʿAbd al-Wahāb Khallāf (1888-1956): A scholar of Hadith, *Uṣūl al-Fiqh*, Comparative *Fiqh* and Inheritance Law. He wrote and published many Islamic books.

• Shaykh Muḥammad Abū Zuhra (1898-1974): A great scholar of *Uṣūl al-Fiqh*, Comparative *Fiqh*, and History. He wrote over 40 books on *Fiqh* and Comparative *Fiqh*, History, Biographies and *Uṣūl al-Fiqh*. He wrote letters to the Shaykh praising him and his works.

HIS COLLEAGUES

The following scholars studied with the Shaykh in Egypt. (*) denotes those who have passed away):

• Shaykh Muḥammad al-Ḥamid (*) from Hama, Syria.

• Shaykh Muḥammad ʿAlī al-Murad (*) from Hama, Syria.

• Shaykh Muḥammad ʿAlī Mishʿal from Homs, Syria.

• Shaykh Maḥmūd Ṣubḥī ʿAbd al-Salām from Libya.

• Shaykh Muḥammad Jamīl Aqqād (*) from Aleppo, Syria.

• Dr. Maḥmūd Fawzī Faydhullāh from Aleppo, currently in Kuwait

The Shaykh has friends beyond count. They were scholars of various backgrounds and specialities, Islamic leaders and activists, to list a few ((*)denotes those who have passed away):

• Shaykh ʿAbd al-ʿAzīz Iuon al-Sud, (*) Homs, Syria.

• Shaykh ʿAbd al-Ghānī ʿAbd al-Khalīq, (*) Egypt.

• Dr. ʿAbd al-Quddūs Abū Ṣāliḥ, a close associate and a dear friend from Aleppo.

• Shaykh ʿAbd al-Raḥmān al-Bānī, who worked with the Shaykh on curriculum of Islamic education in Syria.

• Dr. ʿAbd al-Raḥmān al-Basha, (*) a pious and eloquent writer from Ariha near Aleppo who taught Arabic Literature in Riyadh, Saudi Arabia.

- Shaykh ʿAbd al-Wahāb Altunji, the leading judge at the court of Sharīʿa in Aleppo.
- Shaykh ʿAbdullāh ibn Kanūn, (*) the acknowledged leader of Moroccan scholars.
- Shaykh ʿAbdullāh al-ʿAlī al-Muṭawaʿ, the well known Islamic leader of Kuwait.
- Shaykh Abū ʿAbd al-Raḥmān ibn ʿAqīl al-Ẓāhirī, Riyadh.
- Shaykh ʿAndān Sarmīnī, Aleppo.
- Shaykh Aḥmad Khayrī, (*) faithful student of Shaykh al-Kawtharī.
- Shaykh Aḥmad Sahnūn, (*) Algeria.
- Shaykh ʿAlawī Mālikī, (*) Makkah.
- Shaykh ʿAlī al-Ṭanṭāwī, (*) a judge from Damascus who was known all over the Arab world for his distinguished style in relevant Islamic writings and televised sessions.
- Shaykh Amjad al-Zahawī, (*) Baghdād, Iraq.
- Shaykh Ḥasan Khālid, (*) the Grand Muftī of Lebanon.
- Shaykh Ḥasan Mashat, (*) Makkah.
- Shaykh Isḥāq Azzūz, (*) Makkah.
- Shaykh Khālid al-Madhkūr, the most respected scholar of Kuwait.
- Shaykh Manna' Al-Qattān, (*) a scholar who studied in Egypt and lived in Riyadh.
- Dr. Maʿrūf al-Dawālibī, a native of Aleppo and the ex-prime minister of Syria and the adviser to Kings Faisal, Khālid, and Fahd of Saudi Arabia.
- Shaykh Muḥammad Abū al-Yusr ʿAbidīn, (*) descendant of the great Ḥanafī scholar; Ibn ʿAbidīn. He was a superb medical doctor and a better scholar of *Fiqh*.
- Shaykh Muḥammad al-Ḥabīb ibn al-Khūja, from Tunisia and the

Secretary General of the Islamic *Fiqh* Council, Jeddah.

• Shaykh Muḥammad al-Ḥamawī, (*) a close friend from Damascus who lived and died in Aleppo.

• Shaykh Muḥammad Hamidullāh, a scholar of Indian origin who lived most of his life in humble and austere fashion in Paris. He enjoys vast knowledge of history and other Islamic subjects.

• Shaykh Muḥammad al-Mubārak, (*) Damascus, Syria.

• Shaykh Muḥammad al-Shāmī, (*) Aleppo.

• Shaykh Muḥammad al-Ṭāhir ibn ʿĀshur, Tunisia.

• Shaykh Muḥammad Amīn Quṭbī, (*) Makkah.

• Shaykh Muḥammad Amīn Sirāj, Imām of Fātiḥ Mosque, Istanbul and a close and dear friend.

• Shaykh Muḥammad Maḥmūd al-Sawwāf, (*) originally from Baghdād then immigrated to Saudi Arabia where became an adviser to the King Faisal. One of the outstanding scholars of Iraq.

• Shaykh Muḥammad Nūr Sayf, (*) Makkah.

• Shaykh Muḥammad Saʿīd Ramaḍān al-Būṭī, Damascus, Syria.

• Shaykh Mullā Ramaḍān al-Būṭī, (*) Damascus, Syria. The revered Shaykh was very fond of Shaykh ʿAbd al-Fattaḥ.

• Shaykh Muṣṭafā al-Sibāʿī, (*) Damascus. A close friend and associate in the Muslim Brotherhood movement.

• Shaykh Nadīm al-Jisr, (*) Tripoli, Lebanon.

• Professor Necemettin Erbakan, ex-prime minister of Turkey and a close friend.

• Ustadh ʿUmar al-Amīrī, (*) a close friend and a great poet of Aleppo who lived most of his life in Morocco.

• Shaykh ʿUmar al-Da'ūk, (*) Beirut, Lebanon.

• Shaykh Ṭāhir Khayrullāh, (*) Aleppo, Syria.

- Shaykh Wahbī Sulaymān al-Ghawjī, Damascus, Syria.
- Shaykh Yusuf al-Qaradawi, Qatar.

ACADEMIC WORK IN SYRIA

In 1951, Shaykh Abū Ghuddah returned to Aleppo where he won first place in the teachers' entrance examination and was selected as the principal teacher of Islamic Education. For eleven years, he taught Islamic studies at secondary and religious schools in Aleppo and wrote its curriculum and textbooks. He taught at al-Shaᶜbāniya school, a non-governmental religious school specializing in the disciplines of Islamic knowledge. Then he went to the College of *Sharīᶜa* at the University of Damascus, where for three years he taught *Uṣūl al-Fiqh*, Ḥanafī *Fiqh* and Comparative *Fiqh*. He later directed the production of an Encyclopaedia on Islamic *Fiqh* and also completed a lexicon of the *fiqh* book *al-Muḥalla* by Ibn Ḥazm that had been started by other colleagues and published later by the University of Damascus.

POLITICAL AND DAᶜWA ACTIVITIES

In the 1940's, the Shaykh met with Imām Ḥasan al-Banna in Egypt and joined the Muslim Brotherhood. When he returned to Syria, he was very active in the field of *daᶜwa* and gained the trust of the Muslim masses and elite and the respect of his adversaries. The members of the Muslim Brotherhood in Syria admired and trusted him and eventually elected him as their leader. During his stay in Syria, he was a living school that taught more than three generations of scholars and activists, all of whom were proud to benefit from his vast knowledge. Apart from the weekly sermons that attracted thousands, he held three weekly sessions on *fiqh* questions and answers, on *fiqh*, and on hadith. The Shaykh was very close to the Palestinian cause and participated in many conferences to support it. The late Muḥammad Amīn al-Ḥusaynī (1893-1974) used to visit him every time he visited Riyadh.

In 1962, the Shaykh was elected as a Member of Parliament for Aleppo despite fierce opposition from seasoned contenders. He used this position to help and promote the interests of Islam and Muslims in Syria. In 1966, the military regime imprisoned him for eleven months in Palmyra's military prison with other scholars and politicians before being released during the war of June 1967, when the government released all political prisoners. With him the government imprisoned other Muslim leaders like ᶜĀdil Kanᶜān, Maḥmūd Babillī, Jawdat Saᶜīd, and Marwān Hadid. After his release he remained involved with the Islamic Movement for the rest of his life and enjoyed the admiration and trust of Muslim scholars and the respect of his adversaries and enemies.

In 1978, the Executive Council of *Rābiṭat al-ᶜĀlam al-Islāmī* (Muslim World League) elected the Shaykh to fill Syria's seat that became vacant at the death of the great Shaykh Ḥasan Habanaka.

ACADEMIC WORK IN SAUDI ARABIA

The Shaykh eventually moved to Riyadh, Saudi Arabia where for over twenty-five years he taught at the Higher Institute for Judges, Imām Muḥammad ibn Saud Islamic University and King Saud University. At the Higher Institute for Judges he participated in developing courses and programs. He enjoyed the friendship and trust of many Saudi scholars and officials, notably Shaykh Muḥammad ibn Ibrāhīm al-Shaykh, the Muftī of Saudi Arabia, Shaykh ᶜAbd al-ᶜAzīz ibn Muḥammad al-Shaykh the Rector of Islamic Colleges, Ḥasan ibn ᶜAbdullāh al-Shaykh the Minister of Education, Dr. ᶜAbdullāh ᶜAbd al-Muḥsin al-Turkī, the Rector of Imām Muḥammad ibn Saud Islamic University, Shaykh Ismāᶜīl al-Anṣārī, a great scholar of Hadith.

In Ramadan 1383/1963 he was invited to deliver a lecture at Ḥassanian Lectures sponsored, and attended by King Ḥasan. The lecture focused on explaining a hadith of the Prophet ﷺ and was televised and met with great approval by the King and the

Moroccan scholars. The great scholar of Hadith in Morocco; Shaykh al-Fāsī who was then eighty-seven years old heard the Shaykh's lectures and requested his visit and *ijāzah* in Hadith. King Ḥasan invited the Shaykh to come on numerous other occasions and later awarded him an honorary medal.

In 1976, he taught as a visiting Professor at Umm Durmān Islamic University in Sudan, and in 1978 taught at San'a University in Yemen. He held many teaching sessions and lectures during his visits to scholarly institutions in India, Pakistan, Morocco, Qatar, Algeria, Jordan, Iraq and Turkey. He wrote, edited and published over sixty-five books and left behind about forty books in various stages of writing and editing.

In recognition of his scholarly achievements, Muslim scholars nominated the Shaykh in 1995 for the newly founded Prize of Sultan Brunei for Islamic Studies. The Oxford Centre for Islamic Studies presented the Shaykh with the first award at a ceremony in London attended personally by the Sultan and other scholars and dignitaries.

TRAVELS AND CONTACTS

Shaykh Abū Ghuddah travelled to the following countries: Algeria, Bahrain, Britain, Brunei, Canada, Egypt, France, Germany, Holland, India, Indonesia, Iran, Iraq, Italy, Jordan, Kuwait, Lebanon, Malaysia, Morocco, Pakistan, Palestine (before 1948), Qatar, Somalia, South Africa, Sudan, Switzerland, Tunisia, Turkey, United Arab Emirates, United States, Uzbekistan and the Vatican.

In his travels, he lectured and exchanged knowledge with students and scholars and visited libraries and learning centres of these countries. As a result of his numerous visits to India and Pakistan, and through the numerous tracts and books he had edited and published, he was able to bring much of the knowledge of the Indian Subcontinent to Arab scholars. Among the prominent scholars that he met in these countries were:

- Shaykh Ḥabīb al-Raḥmān al-ʿAzamī (1900-1992): A great scholar and authority of Hadith, *Fiqh*, Biographies and History.
- Shaykh Muḥammad ʿAbd al-Rashīd al-Nuʿmānī (born 1914): A great scholar of Hadith and *Fiqh* living in Karachi, Pakistan.
- Shaykh Muḥammad Shāfi' (1896-1976): A great scholar of *Tafsīr*, Hadith and *Fiqh* and the Muftī of Pakistan, and the father of two great contemporary scholars; Justice Shaykh Muḥammad Taqi Usmani and Shaykh Muḥammad Rafi Usmani.
- Muftī ʿAtīq al-Raḥmān (died 1984): The Muftī of Delhi, India.
- Shaykh Muḥammad Zakariyya Kandahlawī (1896-1982): A great scholar of Hadith and Ḥanafī *Fiqh* who lived his later days in Madinah.
- Shaykh Muḥammad Yūsuf Kandahlawī (1913-1964): The leader of Tabligh-e Jamat in Pakistan and a scholar of Hadith and *Fiqh*.
- Shaykh Muḥammad Yūsuf Binnūrī (1908-1977): A great scholar of *Tafsīr*, Hadith, *Fiqh*, and Arabic Literature and Poetry.
- Shaykh Zafar Aḥmad Usmani (1895-1974): A great scholar of *Fiqh* and an authority on the science of Hadith. Shaykh Zafar Usmani has written a book *'Iʿla al-Sunan* which covers the evidences of the Ḥanafī *Fiqh* based on *aḥadīth*.
- Shaykh Abū'l-Wafā Maḥmūd Shah al-Afghānī (1891-1975): One of the great scholars of this century and an authority on most of Islamic Sciences: Hadith, *Uṣūl al-Fiqh*, *Fiqh* and Comparative *Fiqh*. He edited and published many manuscripts.
- Maulana Abul A'la Maududi (1902-1979): The founder of the Islamic Movement in the sub-continent and the leader of Jamat-e Islami of Pakistan. A great Islamic thinker and writer of many books including a translation of the meaning of the Quran and a *Tafsīr*.
- Shaykh Abul Ḥasan Ali al-Nadwi (1913-2000): A close friend of the Shaykh and a great educationalist scholar who oversaw Nadwat

al-Ulama of Lucknow, one of India's most important institute for Islamic and Arabic studies. A seasoned Islamic leader of India whom Allah blessed with wisdom, knowledge and the love and respect of the people. A native of India of distant Arab descent, who wrote works of Arabic literature better than many Arabs.

GLIMPSES OF HIS CHARACTER

The Shaykh exemplified a distinct noble character combining a scholar and a *Mujāhid*. His knowledge was extensive in its scope and deep in its understanding especially in the fields of *fiqh* [jurisprudence], *Tafsīr* [Quranic exegesis], *adab* [manners], Arabic grammar and literature, history, bibliography, sociology and psychology. His love and concern for the Muslim nation and humanity were great and Allah endowed him with thoughtful insights in his grasp of the challenges facing Muslims. He was polite and gentle in his speech, and when he spoke tears would flow from his eyes with sincerity and humbleness from his heart to touch the hearts of the listeners who would respond with love, respect and trust. His intelligence and quick wit amazed many of his friends and foes.

He was a respectful follower of Imām Abū Ḥanīfa with appreciation and reverence to all Muslim scholars regardless of their school of thought. He was a practical scholar living his time, far from extremism, and would not be reactive or easily provoked. He judged matters in the light of the *Sharīʿa* and taught his students to do the same. An example of this was his stance towards the great scholar, Imām Ibn Taymiyah. Although his teacher Shaykh Muḥammad Zāhid al-Kawtharī made scathing attacks on Ibn Taymiyah and although Shaykh Abū Ghuddah lived and taught in Syria in an environment that was hostile towards Ibn Taymiyah, he would speak respectfully and fairly about him, pointing out the positive aspects of his works and life.

HIS FAMILY

In 1951, the Shaykh married to Sayyidah Fāṭima al-Hāshimī when she was sixteen years old. His marriage was an ideal bond built on love, respect, and dedication for the sake of Allah. His wife for forty six years, Fāṭima al-Hashimi was more than a wife; she was a counsellor, an assistant, administrator, a reader and a researcher. She took care of everything around the Shaykh to enable him to dedicate all his time for serving the religion of Islam. During his sickness, she was always at his side helping without the slightest hesitation or complaint. The Shaykh left behind eleven children, three sons and eight daughters.

HIS RETURN TO SYRIA

In 1995, President Ḥāfiẓ Asad of Syria invited Shaykh Abū Ghuddah, through Shaykh Muḥammad Saʿīd Ramaḍān al-Būṭī, to return to Syria and to meet him. The Shaykh's return in December 1995 was the headlines news for a few days, and was met with great joy and happiness by Syrians who were still holding the Shaykh in great esteem and loved to see him back amongst them. The meeting with President Asad did not materialize though other officials met the Shaykh and were very respectful and cordial.

HIS SICKNESS AND DEATH

In 1973, the Shaykh suffered a heart attack and was hospitalised for a few weeks. However, for the rest of his life, and despite the eventful years he had been through, the condition of his heart was stable. In 1989, the Shaykh complained about deterioration in his sight and doctors at King Khālid Eye Hospital diagnosed it as Macular Degeneration and suggested laser treatment for the retina. The treatment was not very successful but it stopped the disease from spreading further.

In Syria in Shaʿbān 1417/1996, the Shaykh's sight deteriorated again and he decided to go to Riyadh to seek treatment at King Khālid Eye Hospital. The laser surgery was not successful and resulted in sever headache and pain in his eyes. In Ramadan, the Shaykh was hospitalised at King Faisal Specialist Hospital complaining of abdominal pain and internal bleeding. His conditions worsened, and he passed away in Riyadh in the early hours of Sunday the 9th of Shawwāl 1417/16 February 1997. He was buried in al-Bāqī cemetery in Madinah after ʿIshā' prayers of 10th of Shawwāl 1417. Muslims around the world mourned him in Makkah, Madinah, Aleppo, Istanbul, Lucknow, Beirut and Rabat, and his loss was felt most among scholars and students of Islam.

May Allah shower His mercy on him, reward him abundantly and assign him with the Prophets and righteous people for he loved them and mentally lived with them during his long life.

NOTES

1. Reported by Abū Dāwūd in the chapter of *Ṭahāra* [Cleanliness], 1:162, Tirmidhī 1:127 and Imām Aḥmad in *al-Musnad,* 6:256. He stated that ʿĀ'isha reported that the Prophet ﷺ said, "Yes, for women indeed are the counterparts of men." Imām al-Khaṭṭābī said that this means that women are analogous and similar to men in creation, attributes and are subject to the same Islamic rules, unless otherwise specified.

2. Reported by Imām Muslim in the chapter of *Ṭahāra* 3:152. Also reported by Abū Dāwūd, Tirmidhī, Nasā'ī and Ibn Māja in the chapter of *Ṭahāra.* The wording is that reported by Muslim.

3. See pages 3:69 and 4:272.

4. The prominent scholar Imām ʿAbdullāh al-Abdusi al-Fāsī, Imām and Muftī of the city of Fez, Morocco, (died 949 AH), was asked about adding the expression *Sayyidinā* [our master], when the name of our Prophet ﷺ is mentioned in prayers that are quoted verbatim, and those that did not reach us verbatim. Al-Fāsī replied, "Nothing must be added to or omitted from the Prophet's ﷺ original wording. However, if the addition is 'our master' then it is permissible, because the Prophet ﷺ used this expression to teach

his companions when they asked, 'Allah has ordered us to pray for you, how should we pray for you?' On the other hand, if the expressions were not his original wordings, we can add 'our master Muḥammad.'" The great scholar, Imām and Judge Qāsim al-Akabānī al-Talmasānī (died in 854 AH) was also asked this question. He replied, "The best of *dhikr* (remembrances] are those stated in their exact forms by the original propagator of this religion, but mentioning the name of the Prophet ﷺ along with mastery and other glorifying titles is allowed. It is considered an additional worship, especially after the Prophet ﷺ stated that, 'I am the master of the children of Adam'" (Bukhārī and Muslim). Mentioning the Prophet's ﷺ name in its mastery title after receiving this hadith is considered a belief in it. The acceptance of everything the Prophet ﷺ delivered is considered part of worship and faith." (*Al-Mi'ar al-Mu'ārab* by Imām Aḥmad ibn Yaḥyā al-Wanshrīshī, 11:81.)

5. This refers to what travelers place on the back of an animal for the purpose of riding it, decorating it, or for the comfort of the traveler.

6. Muslims should look distinct in their beauty, their cleanness, their nice smell and their good looks, just as some birth marks enhance the beauty of an already nice face.

7. Reported by Muslim in the chapter of *Imān*.

8. As reported by Sahl ibn al-Hanzaliya, cited by Abū Dāwūd 4:349, in the chapter of clothing, and Imām Aḥmad in *al-Musnad* 4:180, and al-Ḥākim in *al-Mustadrak,* 4:183 in the chapter of clothing, the wording here is his.

9. *Majmuʿa Fatāwā* 22:134.

10. Reported by Bukhārī in the chapter of *al-Jumuʿa*.

11. Reported by Bukhārī and Muslim in the chapter of *al-Jumuᶜa.*

12. Reported by Muslim in the chapter of al-*Masājid.*

13. *Arak* or *Siwāk* is a tender branch of the tree Salvadora persica and is used to brush teeth clean.

14. A *Tābiᶜī* is a person who met the Companions of the Prophet ﷺ.

15. See page 1:169.

16. Reported by Muslim in his *Ṣaḥīḥ* in the chapter of *Birr* [Kindness].

17. Reported by Muslim in his *Ṣaḥīḥ* the chapter of *Ashriba* [Drinks].

18. Lived 250-282 AH/864-896CE

19. A *Tābiᶜī* is a person who met the Companions of the Prophet ﷺ.

20. Tirmidhī in the chapter of *Isti'dhān* [Permission].

21. See 1:304.

22. Reported by Muslim in his *Ṣaḥīḥ* in the chapter of *Ashriba.*

23. Reported by Bukhārī in his *Ṣaḥīḥ* in the chapter of *ᶜUmra* and by Muslim in his *Ṣaḥīḥ* in the chapter of *Jihād.*

24. Al-Muwaṭṭa in the chapter of *Isti'dhān* 2:963.

25. Reported by Bukhārī in his *Ṣaḥīḥ* in the chapter of *Isti'dhān* and by Muslim in his *Ṣaḥīḥ* in the chapter of *Adab* [Manners].

26. Reported by Bukhārī in his *Ṣaḥīḥ* in the chapter of *Isti'dhān.*

27. Reported by Bukhārī in his *Ṣaḥīḥ* in the chapter of *Riqāq.*

28. Reported by Bukhārī in his *Ṣaḥīḥ* in the chapter of *Ghusl.*

29. Reported by Bukhārī in his *Ṣaḥīḥ* in the chapter of *Shahādāt* [Testimonies] and by Muslim in his *Ṣaḥīḥ* in the chapter of *Imān* [Faith].

30. See 18:113.

31. Reported by Abū Dāwūd in his *Sunan* in the chapter of *Adab.*

32. Reported by Bukhārī in his *Ṣaḥīḥ* in the chapter of *Isti'dhān* and by Muslim in his *Ṣaḥīḥ* in the chapter of *Adab.*

33. Reported by Muslim in his *Ṣaḥīḥ* in the chapter of *Ṣalāt* [Prayers].

34. Al-Nawawī in *al-Adhkār* in the chapter of *Isti'dhān.*

35. Reported by Bukhārī in his *Ṣaḥīḥ* in the chapter of *Isti'dhān.*

36. Reported by Abū Dāwūd.

37. Ḥāfiẓ Samʿānī, *Adab al-Imala wa'l-Istimla*, 132.

38. Reported by Bukhārī in his *Ṣaḥīḥ* in the chapter of *Taʿbīr* [Expression].

39. Reported by Abū Dāwūd in his *Sunan* in the chapter of *Adab.*

40. Reported by Bukhārī in his *Ṣaḥīḥ* in the chapter of *Isti'dhān.*

41. Reported by Bukhārī in his *Ṣaḥīḥ* in the chapter of *Manāqib.*

42. Reported by Bukhārī in his *Ṣaḥīḥ* in the chapter of *Manāqib* and Muslim in his *Ṣaḥīḥ* in the chapter of *Zuhd* [Abstention].

43. See 1:155.

44. Reported by Bukhārī in his *Ṣaḥīḥ* in the chapter of *Adhān* and Muslim in his *Ṣaḥīḥ* in the chapter of *Ṣalāt*.

45. Reported by Bukhārī in his *Ṣaḥīḥ* in the chapter of *Adhān*.

46. See 1:480.

47. Reported by Bukhārī in his *Ṣaḥīḥ* in the chapter of *Tafsīr*.

48. *Tārīkh al-Islām* 4:197.

49. Ibid 6:213.

50. Ibn ʿAsākir, *Tahdhīb Tārīkh Dimashq*, 7:123 (edited by ʿAbd al-Qādir Badrān).

51. Reported by Bukhārī in his *Ṣaḥīḥ* in the chapter of *Adab* and Muslim in his *Ṣaḥīḥ* in the chapter of *Imān*.

52. Reported by Bukhārī in his *Ṣaḥīḥ* in the chapter of *Adab* and Muslim in his *Ṣaḥīḥ* in the chapter of *Qiṣāma* [Compensations].

53. Reported by Tirmidhī in his *Sunan* in the chapter of *Birr* and Aḥmad in his *Musnad*. Note that the Prophet ﷺ labeled as an outcast a person who does not give the elders their due respect. The importance of such manner cannot be overestimated in life and in social relationships. To ignore this manner is against human nature and is very annoying and frustrating.

54. Reported by Bukhārī.

55. As narrated by Ibn Rajab al-Ḥanbalī, *Zayl Ṭabaqāt al-Ḥanābila*, 1:87.

56. Reported by Bukhārī in his *Ṣaḥīḥ* in the chapter of *Adhān* and Muslim in his *Ṣaḥīḥ* in the chapter of *Masājid*.

57. See 1:46.

58. In his book *Dalīl al-Fāliḥīn ilā Riyāḍ al-Ṣāliḥīn* (2:205), the

eminent scholar Ibn ʿIllān explained this as follows, "Respect of scholars entails honoring them even if they are young. The 'elders' are those who are old in age even if they are not scholars. The dignitaries are those known for generosity, good manners, courage and other noble traits. Precedence is to be given to them over others not enjoying such qualities. You must give them the best seat even if, out of modesty, they do not ask for it. The Messenger of Allah ﷺ used to sit at the nearest vacant seat. Acknowledging their eminence means giving them due respect."

59. This hadith indicates that the wisest be closest to the Imām. This stems from respect. Ibn ʿIllān said, "This distinction is not limited to prayers. In every gathering, the *sunna* is to place the distinguished next to the Imām or the principal. This applies to all types of gatherings and assemblies including lectures and *dhikr*. People are to be ranked according to their degree of knowledge, piety, wisdom, social status, age and competence."

60. This refers to a person who knows the Quran by heart and practices its rules, whereas the deserter of the Quran is a person who abandons reading it and does not implement its commands.

61. See 18:554.

62. See 3:115.

63. In his commentary of *Sharḥ al-Shamā'il*.

64. Reported by Muslim in his *Ṣaḥīḥ* in the chapter of *Ashriba*.

65. The tradition is to call parents by "mother" or "father," and not by their given names.

66. Reported by Muslim in his *Ṣaḥīḥ* in the chapter of *ʿItq* [Emancipation].

67. Reported by Abū Dāwūd in his *Sunan* in the chapter of *Zakāt* and Bukhārī in *al-Adab al-Mufrad.*

68. Reported by Bukhārī in his *Ṣaḥīḥ* in the chapter of *Imān* and by Muslim in his *Ṣaḥīḥ* in the chapter of *Imān.*

69. Reported by Bukhārī in his *Ṣaḥīḥ* in the chapter of *Janā'iz* [Funerals].

70. See 1:604.

71. Reported by Bukhārī in his *Ṣaḥīḥ* in the chapter of *Aṭᶜima* and by Muslim in his *Ṣaḥīḥ* in the chapter of *Ashriba.*

72. Reported by Muslim in his *Ṣaḥīḥ* in the chapter of *Ashriba.*

73. Reported by Abū Dāwūd in his *Sunan* in the chapter of *Aṭᶜima.*

74. Reported by Muslim in his *Ṣaḥīḥ* in the chapter of *Ashriba.*

75. Reported by Bukhārī in his *Ṣaḥīḥ* in the chapter of *Aṭᶜima* and by Muslim in his *Ṣaḥīḥ* in the chapter of *Ashriba.*

76. Reported by Muslim in his *Ṣaḥīḥ* in the chapter of *Ashriba.*

77. Reported by Bukhārī in his *Ṣaḥīḥ* in the chapter of *Aṭᶜima* and by Muslim in his *Ṣaḥīḥ* in the chapter of *Ashriba.*

78. Reported by Tirmidhī in his *Sunan* in the chapter of *Ashriba.*

79. Reported by Abū Dāwūd in his *Sunan* in the chapter of *Ashriba.*

80. Reported by Bukhārī in his *Ṣaḥīḥ* in the chapter of *Ashriba.*

81. Reported by Muslim in his *Ṣaḥīḥ* in the chapter of al-*Thiyāb* [Dress].

82. Reported by Tirmidhī in his *Sunan* in the chapter of *Nikāḥ* [Marriage] and Ibn Māja in his *Sunan* in the chapter of *Nikāḥ.*

83. Reported by Nasā'ī in his *Sunan* in the chapter of *Nikāḥ* and by Ibn Māja in his *Sunan* in the chapter of *Nikāḥ*.

84. This hadith was reported by Abū Dāwūd, Ibn Māja and Tirmidhī in their *Sunan* in the chapter of *Nikāḥ* and authenticated by Ibn Māja and al-Ḥākim.

85. This hadith was reported Bukhārī in his *Ṣaḥīḥ* in the chapter of *Nikāḥ*.

86. This hadith was reported by Bukhārī in his *Ṣaḥīḥ* in the chapter of *Adab*.

87. This hadith was reported by Muslim in his *Ṣaḥīḥ* in the chapter of *Birr*.

88. This hadith was reported by Bukhārī in his *Ṣaḥīḥ* in the chapter of *Maraḍ* [Sickness] and by Muslim in his *Ṣaḥīḥ* in the chapter of *Salām* [Greetings].

89. Examples include, "Get well soon," or "May Allah help you."

90. See 10:276.

91. Al-Ṭabarānī narrated this hadith in his book *al-Manāsik*. The hadith is problematic (*mu'dil*), or attributed (*mursal*) if it is deemed that Al-Muṭᶜim bin Al-Miqdām Al-San'anī heard this hadith from a companion.

92. Al-Dārimī narrated a similar hadith. Ibn Ḥajar ranked it as a fair (Ḥasan) hadith as similar traditions reinforce it.

93. This hadith is a strange and weak hadith that was reported by Ibn Al-Sunnī, Al-Bayhaqī in his book *Shuᶜab Al-Imān*, and *Abū Al-Shaykh* in his book *The Rewards of Deeds*.

94. Ibn al Sunnī narrated this strange hadith.

95. Both hadith are Ḥasan.

96. Al-Tirmidhī narrated this hadith and said it is a fairly authentic hadith.

97. Hadith Ḥasan.

98. Narrated by Abū Dāwūd who ranked it as fair hadith.

99. Imām Muslim reported this without including wealth and children.

100. Al-Nasā'ī narrated this hadith and ranked it as Ḥasan.

101. Reported by Bukhārī and Muslim.

102. Reported by Abū Dāwūd as meeting the conditions of the Muslim.

103. This hadith was reported by Bukhārī in his *Ṣaḥīḥ* in the chapter of *Janā'iz* [Funerals].

104. This hadith was reported by Ibn Māja in his *Sunan* in the chapter of *Janā'iz*.

105. This hadith was reported by Muslim in his *Ṣaḥīḥ* in the chapter of *Janā'iz*.

106. This hadith was reported by Muslim in his *Ṣaḥīḥ* in the chapter of *Janā'iz*.

107. This hadith was reported by Ibn Māja in his *Sunan* in the chapter of *Janā'iz*.

108. This hadith was reported by Bukhārī in his *Ṣaḥīḥ* in the chapter of *Janā'iz*.